The Gift of the Red Envelope

A Guide to Designing Balance, Order and Beauty in Your Home

The Hummingbird is representative of joy, the nectar of life, sense of wonder, life essence, healing power of flowers, infinity, accomplishing that which is impossible, master architects, decorating, creating the joy of home, and playfulness.

Linda Lenore

A Beautiful Center of Light
P.O. Box 7656
Menlo Park, CA 94026
USA

First Printing: April 1998 (The Gift of the Red Envelope)
Revised Printing: August 1999

Library of Congress Cataloging-in-Publication Data
Lenore, Linda
The Gift of the Red Envelope / Linda Lenore
ISBN: 0-9664428-0-6
Library of Congress Catalog Card Number: 99-175856

Printed in the United States of America

Edited by Dina Bensen
Design, production and photography of the book by Paws 4 Art, Menlo Park, CA

Dedication

To Hilory,
My friend, partner, soul-mate
Whose passionate, gentle, and unconditional love for me
has allowed me to soar like a Golden Eagle
and whose grounded connection to
Mother Earth and all that is natural
has given me a solid foundation for building
the presence of God into my life.

And to my children
Melanie,
My daughter and the essence of womanhood
every mother hopes to birth.
Thank you for all the joy and lessons of life we have shared.

Marc,
Who has called me "Mom"
since the moment he asked permission to marry Melanie.
You are the son I longed to have,
I am grateful you are a part of my life.

Jeff,
Whose death gave birth to my deep knowing of God's love,
and whose spirit is with me always.

I am truly blessed by each and every one of you and your presence,
and am grateful to be sharing family life with you
You are the "Heart" of our "Home".

Table of Contents

Acknowledgments

I would like to gratefully acknowledge all the people who have contributed to the completion of this book. To all my women friends in our spiritual networking group who have held me in their prayers through this cycle of life.

And within this circle of light beings, a special thanks to my friend Donnasue who is also the designer and production specialist. Your artistic talents and resources have created a visual image of my dream. Your professionalism is exceed only by your gentle care and love. I will always remember "to get down on all fours and look at life the way my dog, Lay, sees it."

Dina – A lady of many talents (As she puts it, a seven on the anagram) who heard the call of my heart. Your gentle nurturing of my soul through this process allowed me to safely share my stories. Thank you for holding me in the light through this season of my life and for "eye candy".

Irene – Whose knowledge of hers and aromatherapy we will all enjoy weaving into our "simply sacred spaces". May the yellow house soon manifest as The Herbal Home.

Charlene – Who cleared the energy, held the Light and is the Light. Thank you for caring and sharing your intuition, insights and healing processes since our paths came together. I will miss your physical presence as you enjoy Doug, the love of your life.

Carol N. – Thank you for the blessings – the written blessing for our home and for blessing our lives with the many rituals you create from your heart.

Anacaria – Your gentle caring energy was part of the reason I joined NAPO. The first Golden Circle meeting was a wonderful initiation into the "Wild Women with Wisdom". I am honored you allowed me to share your wisdom with others.

Carol M. – We have laughed and cried and shared so many seasons of life together on similar paths. I am blessed to know you and share yet another cycle in our lives.

Melanie – For all those meals you fixed and times you played with the dogs. for all your questions, answers, phone calls, reading, sorting, typing. Once again, you have been an integral part of manifesting my dreams. We make a great team!

Ian – Who held me accountable for my statement it was time to write the book. I had to finish it to continue my part of our dream – the dream of integrating the spiritual into our professional careers.

To all my friends and teachers of life – You are truly "gifts" of the red envelope.

And to Hilory – who encouraged me to write, speak and teach my passion and who maintains the harmony in the house when I am doing it.

Foreword

From the moment I met Linda Lenore, I was fascinated with her story and her wisdom. To be honest, I've always been one for rearranging my knick knacks and spaces. In fact, one of my earliest memories is directing my Mom to "move the bed here and the dresser there" so that it would feel right! For a three-year-old, I sure knew what I wanted even if I wasn't strong enough to move the furniture myself!

Hearing Linda speak gave me a new appreciation of my penchant for moving items around to create a new flow of energy. Now when I spontaneously get the urge, I listen and act! On several occasions I've acted so quickly I ended up laughing out loud when I finally "translated" what part of my home I was so feverishly rearranging or decluttering. I've come to know that just as my dreams and body provide useful information about where I am, the state of my home is also a very telling reflection of my life—a thought that can be both sobering and exhilarating at the same time.

The room that has gone through more transformations, by far, than any other, is my home office. When I first moved into my home, the space that corresponds my Fame area was a concrete slab patio with no, and I mean no, redeeming features. About the time I began writing my first book, *Nature's Wisdom Deck*, I started a remodel project—enhancing the Wealth area and adding my home office. From a logical point of view, the combination of these two projects was insane. Imagine editing a book while a work crew uses a diamond saw to cut away the stucco on the other side of the wall. From an energetic point of view however, the project was completely in alignment with my professional goals. It was during this time that I learned about Feng Shui from Linda and realized the true significance of these enhancements to my home.

Over the years there have been many times when I've been *driven* to rearrange, reorganize, declutter my office-often in the wee hours of the morning I might add. In every case, whether I've known it or not, I've been on the verge of birthing a new project or phase of my business.

In fact, I usually can't make any significant headway with my new ideas *until* I follow my inner guidance. For instance, about three days before I was set to start writing my second book, *The Seasons of Change*, I got that old familiar urge. On a purely logical basis, I had plenty of other tasks I needed to complete before I started my year-long writing project, but intuitively I knew that shifting the energy in my office would have far more impact than any item I could tick off my to-do list. When I was finished — at about two in the morning — I felt the best reward in the world. The energy had shifted so much that I *wanted* to be in my office. A couple weeks into my project, I felt another urge ... this time to write and edit in a different room...my Knowledge area of all places! This arrangement held until about a week after I finished writing and then it was time once again for a shift!

As you read the wisdom Linda Lenore offers in the coming pages, sink into the possibility that subtle shifts in your living and work spaces can open the way for profound changes in your life out in the world. Then as you apply what you learn, open your eyes, ears, and intuition to notice how the "gift of the red envelope" is blessing your life.

Carol L. McClelland, Ph.D.

author of *The Seasons of Change*

Introduction

This book is the result of my many students, clients, and interior designers encouraging me to develop, in written form, my knowledge and experience of Feng Shui, an ancient Asian philosophy/science/art which looks at the relationship and placement of the landscape (mountains, streams, trees and rocks), buildings, floor plans, furniture and accessories and how they affect the human psyche. My first introduction to Feng Shui was not joyful. Yet even while questioning it for years, I found myself incorporating it into my design practice. In doing so, I found clients who loved my designs, their friends who wanted me to "do" their dwellings and offices, and the ability to win awards. Looking back I realize that what I was a blend of common sense, intuition and Feng Shui.

In the past, people used to pay a lot of attention to their home. Mom would be there much of the time making a "honeydo" list for Dad that kept him participating in the mundane items that create that sense of "home". Our lives now, have taken on a craziness that seems to be tearing our society apart. It's not just happening here in the United States, but throughout the technologically developing countries.

It is my feeling that our sense of what is important is out of balance. Interestingly, I have discovered our homes are just as out of balance. When I first started my training in interior design more than 30 years ago, the designs of the houses were much simpler and more balanced from the perspective of the Feng Shui principles. For instance, many of the "tract" homes were square or rectangular in shape creating a floor plan that looks solid and stable. The only "hard" window coverings we had were venetian blinds and shutters, no verticals or mini-blinds. As I go into more and more homes, I am amazed at the lack of knowledge on how to create that sense of "home". Things that I had learned either from a home economics class, or by watching my mother, grandmothers and father, are now lost arts.

Not all parts of home economics classes were important, but at least I knew what to do, when to do it, and how to do it. Using the old adage, "a stitch in time saves nine", it was there that I learned the importance of doing a "little project" quickly or it would turn into a "major nightmare".

Readers of this book will find a combination of interior design "tricks of the trade", Feng Shui and common sense. I cannot emphasize enough the need to use common sense, plus common courtesy. Many a "Feng Shui Cure" has backfired because common courtesy was ignored. For instance, a wind chime in a windy area might keep a person awake all night. Better a wind sock.

Society as a whole has become very self-centered. While it is true we need to do many of these things, like build onto our house because we need more room, we also need to re-member that we do not "own" the world, but are a very small part of it. Maybe adding a second story so we do not need to cut down trees would be a better solution than building out 25 feet and eliminating several large older trees. I always find it works best to practice the Golden Rule of "Do unto others as we would have them do unto us."

The beauty of Feng Shui is that we "Promise never to harm another individual in order to better our own lives." Therefore, we must not take good away from another just to benefit ourselves, but find a way which will be a blessing for all concerned.

In fact, there is even a tradition associated with the aspect of Feng Shui called "honoring the red envelope".

The red envelopes I used while studying this philosophy from the various masters were small Chinese envelops with gold characters printed on them. These are used to wish "good luck, peace, happiness and wealth" to people at various holi-days or special occasions throughout the year – and you can use any type of red envelope. "Honoring" the red envelope is a practice used at the end of each class to: 1) thank the teacher for the knowledge they have given so freely and graciously, 2) to promise to use it only for good and never to harm another human being, especially for our own gain, 3) to realize the importance and power behind the giving and receiving of knowledge, 4) to share the information only with those who ask and who promise also to use it appropriately, and 5) to closely guard the "secret" information of this oral tradition so the honor, power and integrity of this oral philosophy would be maintained.

The number of red envelopes and the amount of money placed inside would vary each time depending on the number of "blessings" or "ceremonies" we were taught during the class. Sometimes the number or amount of money requested or offered would be symbolic, following the customs of this Asian art.

In the beginning for me, bringing the philosophy of Feng Shui (which suggests using beads in doorways if you did not have a door) into interior design, AND MY LIFE, was very problematic. Many of the principles of Western design seemed to be in direct conflict with the Eastern way of Feng Shui, as was the case with those beads. I might have been able to get away with it back in the 60's, especially in some areas of San Francisco, but we were now in the early 80's. Also, it was a time in my life where I was fighting inside . . . inside at the core of me. Who was I? What do I believe? What am I about? What do I really want in life? Is this the life I want to continue or is there more? Could it really be that life could be summed up with the statement, "The one with the most toys wins?"

I thought not. But it meant I would have to rethink and redo most, if not all, of my own life!!!

And if I were to "redo" my life, my practice of "selling products" in the design industry as the way to generate income would also have to be rethought. Did I want to do that? Was it time to do that? Did I trust that I would be able to find a way to survive economically?

Then I questioned, so what is survival? Is it merely existing day by day, from paycheck to paycheck? Or is it "Maslow's theory of the basics of food and shelter?" If survival is about shelter, maybe there WAS a connection in all of this.

Would it follow that by doing my shelter I would be redoing my life? I knew my life changed when I got married and moved 400 miles. There were new neighbors, different stores to shop at and a different climate.

When a child is born into the family, there is a whole new energy around it. The den may become the baby's room. That extra dresser you had for yourself might be painted and moved to the baby's room. What causes the change in our lives – is it the baby or the furniture, or is it both?

What about the forced changes that occur with a health challenge? When my mother was ill and she had to be moved into a facility. I looked for an environment that was most "like home" so as to reduce the amount of stress and anxiety she would go through.

Which brings us to the next question: what defines a "home"? For one person it might be a cozy studio apartment, rather austere in nature, another person might want a farm in the country, and a third the mansion in the Hollywood Hills. Or it could be a track house where they all look alike except for the color.

Each person it is different. Just as I was asked today, "Is it better to paint the door red or black?" The answer lies within the individual or occupants of the dwelling. According to Feng Shui, either one might be appropriate to increase one's career activity. Red might be better for one person and black for another.

So how do you know when your surroundings are right for you? Ultimately, only you will know. For we may paint the door red and you will love it. But the neighbors might complain too "loud" for the neighborhood. Or you find that more solicitors stop at your house, whereas before, they started down the block and gave up before they reached your house; now you are constantly being bothered, perhaps feeling invaded, and getting less done.

Each of us is different and each of our choices make different things happen. We go through different cycles in our lives, different cycles within the hour, day, week, month, season, year. For instance, the choice to attend college may result in a Monday, Wednesday and Friday class so you have to get up earlier for days during the quarter. You will have a different routine on those days than others. When you are expecting a baby, you may sleep more the first trimester, have energy the second, and move at a slower pace in-between the second and third trimesters. You get the picture.

So, here are some guidelines on what to do. These are just guidelines. Some that have withstood the test of time. Yet we may find that the environment we live in will not allow us to follow all of them because you may line in a house or apartment with CC&R's (Covenants, Conditions and Restrictions). Then we have to get creative. That is a gift we have been given – the gift of "Choice".

If you live in a condo, these rules have been setup to maintain a sense of commonalty within the complex. Often these are very good, unless they have been set up only to reduce cost and limit personalization. Then they could be limiting the individual and their potential to achieve. We do not have to fight to change the CC&R's. There are many ways we can raise the awareness of the members of the board on the psychological impact the exterior of our dwellings plays in our lives. Educating the Boards in these complexities usually will improve their understanding and allow the changes to occur. There are many ways to change and enhance the exterior of these multi-unit communities that actually build a sense of camaraderie.

There are many people who say there is bad Feng Shui and that you can not fix it unless you tear down the house or remodel. I do not believe this is true. Some of the books tend to create fear In people who read them. They become uncomfortable in their homes. They think they have to do the remodel or tear it down or move. If they can't afford to do any of those, they begin to live in fear of their home space.

IS THIS WHAT FENG SHUI IS ALL ABOUT? TO DISEMPOWER AN INDIVIDUAL IN THEIR OWN HOME? NO!!! I think not.

The HOME is a refuge. Very possibly it is the only place of safety we know. Is this ancient philosophy really going to imply that your life is working against you because you don't have it all perfect, that your house is responsible for your "Bad Luck?" Again, the answer is NO!

What is does mean is that there are times when you can use a blending of the knowledge to improve your life. Build upon it. Do the things that make sense for you to do now. Leave the rest. If one of the items calls to you to do it later, or in a different way. FOLLOW YOUR GUT! TRUST IT!!!

This book is not a complete book on all aspects of interior design. It is a guide for you – to help you with ideas to blend our Western design, beliefs, and way of living with this ancient philosophy that originated in China. Many of the ideas are universal, so I will not say "This is Feng Shui" unless I feel it is necessary. Some of it is basic design while other parts are in direct conflict to some of the principles of Western design. You will need to make decisions as to which approach you want to take throughout this book.

And this book is much more. It is meant as a opening up to the deeper meaning of our dwellings. They contain symbology, significance, and sacredness in how our everyday lives transpire. It will not give you the "quick fix" solution, only suggestions and guidelines to open your awareness of the environment, especially YOUR environment.

My hope is that my struggle with this ancient philosophy/ science/art will make your life more of what you desire your life to be. I hope these years of creating "Home" for others will help you to create your own "HOME".

In Love and Light,
Linda Lenore

The Gift
of the
Red Envelope

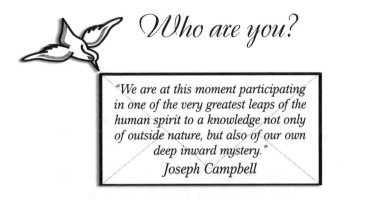

Who are you?

> "We are at this moment participating
> in one of the very greatest leaps of the
> human spirit to a knowledge not only
> of outside nature, but also of our own
> deep inward mystery."
> Joseph Campbell

In Western society, it has traditionally been the role of women to create the nurturing space called home. We had the responsibility to choose what furniture was needed, where it was to be placed, and when and where to add accessories. We would often have help with this process from family and friends since we lived in community with them. Sometimes this extended family would do a "barn raising" for the community's newly married couple, or hand-craft a piece of furniture in celebration of this or other special occasions.

When the industrial revolution occurred, more and more people moved away from the towns where they were raised. Furniture became less expensive as machines could turn out items in quantity. In wartime, more women worked away from home. It was at this time we started to move away from homelife as a focus, and we lost sight of the intricate role the home played in our lives.

No longer were several generations living closely together where they could learn, share and care for one another. Wars had taken fathers, uncles, and brothers, and it was up to women to leave the home and work. Women's connection to home began to decline further. Another change occurred. As college education became more valued than being a "housewife," and since so many women had gone through the educational system without being trained in how to be a "homemaker," the image and sense of home became a lost art.

What I find to be fascinating, is that now, when we are beginning to realize the importance of home in our overall life picture, there is an emergence of an Ancient Chinese philosophy (Feng Shui) which directly relates to this issue and answers the question, "What is a good home?" Then added to this "coincidence," is the fact that our technology allows us to travel globally through the Internet while we are "working at home," and I become amazed at its far reaching implications.

It is my belief that we have the potential within each of us to change many of the world's challenges by creating peace and harmony within our home. It may not happen over night, but slowly ripple through each community until the shift in energy is felt around the world.

If there is righteousness in the heart,
There will be beauty in the character.
If there be beauty in the character,
There will be harmony in the home.
If there is harmony in the home,
There will be order in the nation.
And if there be order in the nation,
There will be peace in the world.

Confucius

As you learn of the many implications the building we call "home" has on our personal success, relationships, health, and finances, and since most people say they would like to improve at least one of these areas in their lives, I believe that you will see the potential also.

Before you start to change the interior of your living space, whether you are designing a home, condo, or apartment, it would be good to get to know more about yourself, the interior of you.

This is an adventure, an adventure to discover who you are, where you are going, and is there anyone with you?

What styles do you like and dislike? What is the function of the room? Who is going to be using the room? How much time will be spent there? What time of the day will it be used? What "feel" do you want? If you have pets, will they be in the room? Will there be young children, elderly, or a disabled person using the space?

Even more important than some of the above questions are the questions we don't often ask ourselves. How do I see myself? Am I a soft and gentle soul, or am I very "hard shelled?" Do I want others to know about me when they enter my space, or do I want a shield around me, a facade that makes people think I'm something different?

Am I willing to show the world what I'm truly made of? Do I need to keep up an "image?" Does it include being surrounded by lots of expensive items, or do I like simplicity? You need to know if you are trapped into believing you **need** objects around you so that people will think you're somebody important.

These are tough soul searching questions that I have asked myself as well as my clients. It's important to "get real."

Before we go any further, I'd like to share with you something I learned from one of my clients. At our first appointment, I asked her to make a list of the ideal outcome she would like in her home. A few days later she called to cancel the appointment, saying she needed more time. About a month later I received a 9"x12" manila envelope with 20+ pages with the smallest type, single-spaced, computer-generated list of what she desired in each of her rooms.

She knew it was physically impossible to do most of the list in this house, but she had spent the time writing it down so it became clear to her. Many of the items she had never mentioned to her husband. Now she was able to express her vision of their home, and with her list in front of him, he was able to add his thoughts also. Their combined effort resulted in a four year project which brought them closer in their relationship because they learned to share with each other their deepest desires.

Some of these deep desires stem from the things we concluded were "safe," "nurturing," "comfortable," or "necessary" as a child. It takes time and a willingness to discover these, but you will reap wonderful rewards for your effort.

Your home needs to embody the essence of you. Often this requires one to journey into areas you've never before ventured. You may not be ready or willing to do this at this time. Give yourself permission to read over each exercise and decide if you're ready. If not, simply skip to one that appeals to you. You can always return to an unexplored area at some later date. If you **are** ready to explore this area, let me give you some ideas.

What does your "nurturing spot" look like?

When you were a child, and things didn't go right, what did you do?

As a small child, most of the time when I was upset, I would storm off to my room, slam my door shut, and throw myself onto the bed. Then one of my parents would come into the room, scold me, and leave. This only made things worse. So as a got older I learned to find a place to hide where no one could find me. I had several, some inside the house, some outside. I found in designing my homes, I needed to recreate those same "safe, nurturing" areas around my dwelling. And so do you.

The following questions are to help you remember those locations from the past, and help you define the qualities which are important for your soul to feel protected. There are beautiful gemstones hidden in these questions. Look for the sparkle in your smile and the light in your heart. Pay attention as your inner energy shifts from thoughts to feelings. The outer to the inner. From doing to being. Now ask yourself:

Where did I go to get nurtured?

Was it inside or outside?

Is it easy to get here?

Do I have several places?

Do these places have anything in common?

Am I at a friend's house?

Are there adults there?

Are there children?

Are there family members around?

Am I alone?

Am I wearing some special article of clothing? If so, what color is it? Does it have a fragrance? What shoes am I wearing?

Are there toys with me or a blanket? What color is the blanket? Does it have a name? Describe it!

Am I in a room or closet?

What colors are these?

Is it large or small?

Is it light or dark?

Does it have a window?

More than one?

Do I notice any odor or smells?

Is there any furniture?

Am I sitting in a chair or rocker?

Is someone holding me?

Is it daytime or nighttime?

Is there a noise, the sound of music, a train, or children in a nearby school yard?

Is there wallpaper on the wall? What color, pattern?

Am I out-of-doors? In a field or meadow? By a creek? In a cave?

Is the temperature . . . hot, cold, clammy, sweltering?

What time of the day is it . . . early morning, late morning, afternoon, evening?

Have I been here at this time of the day before?

Is there anything growing nearby? Flowers? Trees? Bushes? I know the names of them? Do I like them?

Am I lying in the grass? Does it feel soft? Is it freshly cut? Is there a hill? Can I roll down it? Do I like to roll down it?

Is there an activity I am doing? Fishing? Sewing? Reading?

Am I very active or very quiet or somewhere in between?

Is this my "private" space? Does anyone else know where it is? Can people find me? Am I with other people? Can I be left alone if I want to be while I'm in this space?

I find it incredibly helpful for my clients to spend time going through these questions. We rarely think about our childhood and how we survived. Many of us had very difficult times. Others of us were blessed to have really wonderful, sensitive families. We each had experiences that filled our body, mind, and spirit with the tools we need today to live the quality of life we want and deserve. By digging deeper into the "ground," our roots, we find what served us as children. Then we can build our homes with a solid foundation laid on bedrock, a very stable base on which to construct, and we will add the framework that will contain our hopes, dreams and desires of life.

Here's what I do when I want to discover more ideas to nurture me:

First, I make certain I will be alone. I like to lie down on the sofa near where the stereo is located, and I put on a couple of soft-music CD's (I have several favorites). There's some popcorn nearby and a cup of herbal or green tea, possibly with honey. Of course, the phone is unplugged, and the door is closed. I have a cat who loves to curl up on my lap and purrs whether I scratch her neck and ears or not. There are several candles lit; some are special fragrances or aromatherapy.

After I have nurtured myself like this for awhile, I will let my mind drift to an earlier time and place where I had the same feeling I have at this moment. What do I remember? I write this down in a journal. These are symbols that have meaning in my life.

Included in this list are:

Lattice and picket fences

Arbors with roses growing over them
Iceland poppies
Brick fireplaces and barbecues
Curved used brick walkways
Daffodils
Narcissus
Grassy knolls
Fuzzy blankets
Cats
Stuffed animals
White painted 6-paneled doors
Riding my bike to far away places
Elm trees

There may be some things from the more recent past which call to me as well, like bay windows, redwood trees, and fish ponds.

Do you know how to nurture yourself? Do you have a ceremonial place or ritual you have created to take care of yourself? Have you ever taken a bath with soft music and candles? Does the thought of curling up by the fireplace on a cold wintry day in a big overstuffed chair with a quilt or blanket remind you of your childhood?

What symbolizes deep nurturing and caring for you? How can we build that into your home or apartment? Write down any thoughts you have whenever you get them. Write them in the margins. Have a stack of bright colored Post-it notes by the desk at work, the phone by your bed, and in the car. I just found a multicolored, almost fluorescent, spiral pad that I love. Whenever you get ideas, write them down.

Inspiration comes like a shooting star, day or night. Sometimes we see it, many times we don't. But I can assure you, you will most probably forget it if you don't write it down. There is power, an energy, in writing it down. Get fun pens to write with also. Sometimes nontraditional colors or novelty pens will bring you joy and brilliant ideas.

Having started the process of nurturing yourself, I'd like you to think about the things that are most important to you.

We want to find meaning in your life. Remember, this book is a guide for you to develop a home that embodies the essence of you, not an image or facade you have been living and projecting for years. Your home will change as you become more aware of who you are, connecting to your "authentic self," as Sarah Ban Breathnach says it in her book, *Simple Abundance*. This is a wonderful book to explore more of who you are.

So again, what has meaning in your life? What really matters? in Feng Shui, the Ba-Gua (Ba-Gua which means "eight sides" and gives us the form we use to help us locate the nine energy areas of our life) is often used to give guidance. It contains nine areas of life that are thought to be represented in the physical dwelling. If they are represented and balanced in the physical dwelling, then one's life will also be balanced and complete. We will go into a more definitive discussion of the Ba-Gua in a later chapter, but for now those nine areas might give you some ideas to contemplate.

Aspects of the nine areas are: finances, profession, education, spouse, children, health, parents, friends, and integrity.

Think for a minute while looking around your living space to see if you can find items that remind you of these nine areas. Now go to another room in your house or your office to see how well the representation is in that room.

We have a tendency to have many items associated with one or two areas of our life in a room, but rarely all of them. Sometimes we have nothing grounding us depicting one certain aspect of our life. How sad this is, not to be acknowledging an essential part of our being.

For instance, I often go into a client's environment where I find only books. No family photos. Or into a living room where there is nothing but family photos. No books or professional representation. I don't believe this means we need to have more "stuff" in each room. We just need to realize that what we see every day plays a major role in how we feel about ourselves and how we view our world. Is it just for "show?" Is it "all work and no play?" Or all geared for material items with no regard to "financial responsibility?"

As I said before, this is not the typical design book that purports the need to have "all the right stuff," but rather one that will guide you to make choices which reflect who you are or what you want to be, deep within your soul.

What is your style?

Next we need to find out what attracts your attention and what style you are and/or love. We're not talking about the seasonal style and coloring. We're referring to the life you have lived and the one you want to live. What are your dreams? Can you imagine the most wonderful life and environment you could possibly have?

I grew up seven miles from downtown Los Angeles. My father, an engineer for the Southern Pacific railroad, usually worked the "graveyard shift" from midnight to 8:00 a.m. My mother would take me to "the yards" once a week at three in the morning to have "lunch" with my father. Sadly, the only vacations we were able to take before he died were just two, one to the Grand Canyon and next to Bryce National Park.

My childhood nurturing experiences had more to do with nature and nighttime than other children. I had very limited knowledge of the cultures of the world and the locations where we would eat were usually coffee shops, little Mom-and-Pop Mexican restaurants, and the early morning bakeries that my father got to know throughout the years he drove through town to work.

My home environment remembrances consist of Mexican pottery, bright colored blankets, sombreros, bakery utensils, and railroad memorabilia. When I married a man who had a similar background, we designed our first home using those types of items.

Later on, as I traveled and learned about other styles and cultures, I yearned to revisit those areas of Bryce and the Grand Canyon. I was drawn to the red rock areas. Through college and my early 20's, my preferences did change, little by little.

I still like a homey kitchen and train memorabilia, but the Mexican sombreros have changed to more of the Southwest feel, including the rich New Mexico sunset colors, and incorporating the colors of the red rock landscapes. Also, I have added the work of artists I admire, Zen artifacts, and antiques I have fallen in love with.

So as you can see, we want to know what has appeal to us and why. Sometimes we are drawn to a style without the tools to understand why. If you explore through this process, you will most probably discover a "pearl of great price."

If there is more than one person occupying the space, it would be beneficial for them to participate also. Sometimes this is not workable for any number of reasons. If that is the case, it would be a good idea if one person would take it upon themselves to look for pictures of various examples they like, then show these to the other and begin a discussion around the pictures. This will open a dialogue with all possibilities open and available.

Start by getting several magazines or ads from newspapers and be willing to cut or tear out everything you like and dislike. Label it with post-it notes or write on it to express your feelings. It's a good idea to make a note at which store you can find it, in case it's something you love and might want to purchase later.

This is a time to let go of the logical mind. Go sit in that comfortable chair. Get in a meditative or dreamy state. Play as if this were fantasy time. Anything goes! The more outrageous, the better. This is an expedition into your heart and soul. How would you create "home" if you had all the money possible and no other responsibilities or restrictions? This can be very rewarding. We'll think about our budget later. For now, dream on!

Don't forget to write down any thoughts you have on places you've been or names of styles you know you like. Sometimes we can't find the pictures and yet we have the image. Describe it the best you can. Get the feel of it.

Painting the Picture

What do you see? How do you feel?

> **Painting the Picture**
> *"Paint the picture from your soul,*
> *Watch it manifest like a goal"*
> Linda Lenore

We are now going to venture into the world of make believe. We are going to live like a fairy tale princess and paint the picture of our dreams. We may not have answers or images for all of these questions. But the more focusing we do, the more clear the picture becomes.

When you have a chance, this step will give you still more insights into who you are, what you want in this world, and what you believe. It will help you realize part of your ancestral heritage* — a part of you which came from stories you heard from family or friends, books or articles you have read, and dreams that came to you during the day or night. Something resonates within you when you bring these insights into focus. As you allow your soul — that small unit of energy that defines who you are, that essence of you as a person — to reveal these gifts, you will imagine a spark of energy deep within you that starts glowing like embers, shining a bright light inside you. You are awakening your soul! It is calling to you.

"Kasu" is the Japanese word used to describe the feelings a person gets when a house calls to them. Do you know what your soul yearns for in the creation of home? Does it speak to you in your dreams? During the day, do you sometimes find yourself thinking of it? Can you describe it?

*Carl Jung has called this the "collective unconscious."

Go through each step, letting the questions prompt your memory. Look at the images you have cut out from the magazines. Do they trigger emotions? Fond memories? Laughter?

Where else does your mind wander? What joy is uncovered? Can your little child come out to play? So again I say, "Kasu, What calls to you?"

Where you live:

Where is your "home" located? In a high-rise building? On a country lane?

What does the street look like?

Is your building unique? The only one on the block like it? Or does it blend into everyone else's on the block?

Does it have a name?

What color is it? Is it many colors?

Does it have a particular style?

What's the shape? Location? Building material?

Any unique architectural features?

Approaching the entrance:

Do you have a walkway? With lights? Flowers?

Is there a garden? Trees? Fountains?

Is there a porch? Swing? Chairs and tables?

Can you see the front door from the street?

What does the door look like? Is it wood? Painted? Glass?

What kind of handle do you have?

Is there a door bell? Brass knocker? Small chimes?

Are there stained or beveled glass side lights?

A wreath on the door?

Statue by the door?

A real dog curled up on the porch?

Opening the front door:

What is the first thing you see? A mirror? A scenic view?

Are you entering the foyer? Living room? Kitchen?

Is there a plant? Vase of flowers? Fountain or aquarium?

Can you walk straight into a room? Is there a partial wall?

Do you have a place to set your keys? Mail? Purse?

How do you feel when you enter this space? Safe? Energized?

Do you want to stay right here? Walk through it? Leave? Move to another room?

Do you have a greeter? An angel? Carousel horse? Wooden giraffe? Buddha? Quan Yin?

The living room/family room/great room:

Is it large, able to hold lots of people? Or small, suitable for intimate gatherings?

Are the walls painted? What color?

Is there wallpaper? What pattern?

Any moldings? Around the doors? Crown? Wainscoting?

Fireplace? What material? Mantel?

Windows? How many?

Window coverings? Hard coverings, as in blinds or shutters? Soft coverings, as in curtains and drapes?

Is there one place for conversation or many?

How many sofas do you see?

Do they match? Is it a sectional?

Are they all upholstered or part wood?

Is it oversized? An antique? Traditional or modern?

Is the fabric soft to the touch? Is it leather? What color?

Is there a pattern to the fabric?

Are there pillows? A few or many? Do they all match in pattern and color or are they unique unto themselves? Are they attached to the back or detached?

How many chairs?

Are they small, medium or large? Wood? Upholstered? Metal? Combinations? What is the fabric like?

Does it match the sofa, other chairs, a table skirt, or the drapes?

Do they have clean lines? Modern or shaker styling? Ornate? Antique? Pillows? Rocker, swivel, combination, stationary, recliner, or with ottoman? High back or low back?

Any tables?

End tables? Lamp stand? Sofa table? A game table? Coffee table?

What do they look like? What material? Wood? Metal? Plastic? Glass? Leather? Tile? Library table?

What other furniture is in the room?

Armoire? TV, stereo, or entertainment center? Speakers? Tea cart? Desk? Curio cabinet? Etagere? Bookcases? Fountains? Aquarium?

What kind of lighting?

Floor? On tables? Wall sconces? Up lights? Hanging? Cantilever? Ceiling cans?

What flooring?

Carpeting? Hardwood? Tile? Painted or stained concrete?

Accessories and what else?

Plants? Artwork? Statues? Pottery? Area rugs? Quilts? Stuffed animals? Candle holders (wall, floor or table top)? Blankets?

Collections?

A weaving loom? Spinning wheel? Potters wheel?

A large black panther? A playful dolphin?

Kitchen:

How big is it? Do you like an intimate, easy to use space?

Is there more than one person in the kitchen at a time?

Is there more baking than cooking? Or is it equally distributed?

Do you like to entertain? Is the entertaining done around meals?

Are they formal meals or informal gatherings?

Is it part of a great room? Eating nook?

Do you like a very clean, almost sterile feel?

Do you like the feel of a galley or gourmet cook type kitchen?

What type of cabinets do you want?

What kind of doors? Wood? Metal? Glass?

Is it contemporary in feel? Possibly European?

Simple or with all the "bells and whistles?"

Do you like everything out where you can see it? Everything behind doors? A combination?

What shape do you prefer? U-shaped? Square? What kind did your mother have? Did you learn to cook there? How did it work for you? Would you be able to work in one like it now?

Does it have a window? Does it look out at the front yard? Backyard? Courtyard? A park? Atrium? Another view? What kind of treatment on them? Blinds? Shutters? Curtains? Valance? Combination?

What color are the walls? The cabinets? The floor?

Does it have wallpaper? What color is it? What pattern?

What type of floor?

Vinyl? Wood? Tile?

What type of cabinetry?

What finish is the counter? Formica? Tile? Corian?

What type of sink? Steel? Porcelain? Corian? Double? Single? Special combination? Do you need two sinks?

A large or small stove? Gas or electric? Induction? More than one stove?

Gas or electric oven? Convection? Microwave? One? Two? Three? More? Different types?

Barbecue or rotisserie?

What kind of dishwasher? Need two?

Multiple sinks, multiple garbage disposals?

Is there art work? Pottery? Pictures? Baskets? Copper? Brass? Plates? Plants? Fruit?

Clear counters? Lots of objects on the counter? Cutting blocks?

How about a pantry?

Mickey Mouse and Donald Duck memorabilia?

Aunt Jemima dolls and Log Cabin Syrup containers?

Do you have special needs? Is someone disabled? Do you want to plan for the possibility that someone who is disabled might want to use the kitchen? Are you or is your family tall? Would you like to have the counters tall enough so you don't have to lean over? Are you petite? Would a few counters at a lower height be more comfortable?

Eating/Dining rooms:

Where do you eat? Is it a formal dining room? Is it part of the kitchen? At a counter?

Are there windows? Does it get morning or afternoon light? Is it direct sun or diffused lighting?

Do the windows have curtains? Blinds? Drapes? Nothing? Combinations?

Is there a table? How big? What style? Wood, Formica, brass, or glass?

How many people can sit there? Two? Four? Eight? More?

Is there one eating spot for morning and one for evening?

Are there two locations to eat—one formal, one informal? Is it inside, but feels like its out-of-doors?

Is it in the center of the house with no windows?

Does it look dark there? Are the walls paneled? Does it feel nurturing to you?

What do the chairs look like? Are they wood? Painted or stained? Metal? Fabric? Rattan? Wicker? Wooden seats? With cushions? Vinyl?

Is there other furniture? A Baker's rack? China cabinet? Buffet? Breakfront? Tin pie rack cabinet? Tea cart? Hutch? Butcher's block?

What does the lighting look like? Is it canned ceiling lights? A Tiffany shade? Crystal chandelier? Modern? Traditional? Wagon wheel? Halogen? Ceiling fan?

A doll high chair? Miniature tea set? A 50's diner with juke box?

Your bedroom:

Are you alone here or do you share it with someone else?

What size is the bed?

Does it have a headboard? Foot board? Four-poster?

What do they look like? Wood? Wicker? Rattan? Lacquer? Metal? Brass?

Is there a quilt, afghan, or down comforter? Dust ruffle? Full or partial canopy? No pillows? Lots of pillows?

Is there a night stand? More than one? Do they match? Different? Modern? Antique? Small? Large? Made to be a night stand or something unique? Bedside wash table? With bowl and pitcher?

Any mirrors? Full wall? On closets? Free-standing? Round? Oval? Above the dresser?

Is there a dresser? Armoire? Wood? Lacquer? Partially glass? Mirror doors? No doors?

Any bookcases? Filled with books? Some books? Displays pictures? Curios?

A desk? For writing or household bills? Computer? What kind? Roll-top? Drop leaf? Metal and glass? Wood? Marble top?

Chairs, ottomans, or benches? To go with the desk? To put on shoes? To hang the quilt over? Wooden? Upholstered? To watch TV? Curl up in to read? Watch a fire?

Does it serve other activities? Exercise? Reading? Meditation?

Do you want a stereo? Water fountain? Plants? Vanity? Doll house? Stuffed animals? Aquarium? Art? Statues? Icons or religious figures? Big tufted, overstuffed ottoman or vanity stool?

Are there toys for the inner child? Raggedy Ann and Andy? Betty Boop? Ken and Barbie? A big stuffed polar bear? An ape hanging from the ceiling? A rocking horse? Snoopy and Red Baron flying a bi-plane?

Bedrooms for the children:

Do you want a single bed? Bunk beds? Trundle?

Is it made into a tree house? Or a boat, car, or bus?

Is the flooring carpet, wood, or tile? Is there an area rug which looks like a town with a road and railroad tracks? Does it look like the playing board of the game Monopoly?

Do the closets become puppet stages? And the dressers castles?

Is it an airplane hanger? A "Wild West" town?

Is it a zoo or "Alphabet Soup"?

Is the ceiling painted blue with white clouds? And will you add the glow-in-the-dark stars and solar systems so it comes alive at night?

What did you want as a child or what have you wanted as a grown-up for your inner-child? Can you create it in your child's room or some other part of the home?

What might you like in your bedroom? How about that big stuffed bear in your bedroom? Or the underwater scene with the whale? Or the mother tiger playing with her cubs painted on your bathroom wall?

Bathrooms:

What style? Funky 50's? Deco 30's? Grecian Spas?

What color? White and add bright towels? Color tiles?

Shower for two? Whirlpool tub? Look like a waterfall? Part of the out-of-doors?

Dark and cozy?

Light and bright?

What were you thinking and feeling while answering these questions? Did past memories of your childhood come to mind? Did you remember a kitchen where food and love were equally fed to you? Were dreams of long ago brought back to life?

I think I have always been very visual, for as a child I would have lots of dreams I could remember. Some were nightmares. Many were not. But there was one which reoccurred for most of my childhood and adult life about a yellow house with white shutters, a picket fence, and a duck pond. I actually only "saw" this house in my dreams until one day while traveling in another country, I saw that house!!! It was real! I just couldn't believe it. But my heart and soul knew instantly what I had found. I recognized my "home."

I'm not saying to you that I have lived there in this life or any other. What I am saying is that deep within my Being there was a realization that the essence of this place connected with the essence of me. It just so happened that I was at a particularly low point in my life, and by seeing this house, then, I was made more conscious of what I needed to do, now. What I needed to do was not only create my "home," but I needed to build the kind of life around it that I wanted to live. This was the message. To trust in my dreams – **and they would become reality.**

So, I ask you, what is the picture your heart and soul wants painted? What is the essence of each room for you? How can your "home" support your dreams?

Look at these pictures often. Make a collage by putting them together on a piece of paper. If you have room or want to display them, put them on a large piece of poster board or form core. This is the map to your dreams – **your treasure map, the map to your dreams becoming reality!**

Enter Thy Holy Temple: The Essence of Home

Deep inside this structure we call home, there lies incredible meaning to the soul. We know we need to go home to recuperate from a major trauma such as surgery. We know it is a place to care for our young. After a long day's work, we go home to sleep and rest the tired body. So, we know it is a place to nurture our physical bodies. But what about the mental, emotional, and spiritual parts of us? What role does it play in those aspects of our lives?

We have famous sayings like "Home is where the heart is", Be it ever so humble, there's no place like home", and "A man travels the world in search of what he needs and returns home to find it". Why are such things written about this structure called "home", and why don't we talk about our work environments with such love and care?

First, "home" is natural – from nature; "work" is not. Thousands of years ago, we did not have careers or professions. We had jobs. The jobs were to find shelter and food in order to live. We're talking basic survival – the jobs of hunting, fishing, scouring for food. And then having a barrier between you and the elements – shelter, a home, a natural part of life.

What did shelter look like back then? It might have been just a tree for shade from the sun. But at night when predators were looking for food, it would be a cave or hollowed out spot in the truck of a tree. Then perhaps, as Indian lore states, "the Great Spirit directed antelope to teach man how to use skins from animals to help protect man from the elements."

I feel the second reason we don't have wonderful sayings about work, as we do about home, has to do with nurturing — the love, care, inspiration, roots, and a place to call our own, a connection that we need as human beings.

When I teach my classes, I get the same comments. They have to do with the "feelings" people have regarding their home or apartment. They reveal the innate desire to build, create, develop, share, and change within the dwelling. They say things like:

"I have always wanted to do this to my home."

"It just seemed right for me to put the table under the window instead of by the sofa."

"I had a plant in one spot, but it didn't feel right there, so I moved it. It's made a world of difference."

"I thought I was crazy to want to paint the wall red (or blue or purple or whatever color). Then after I took your class, I painted it the color I've dreamed of. It's what I've always wanted to do, and I feel more alive now that I've done it."

"I didn't know why I liked this one spot in the house more than any other until you talked about the different energies within our homes. I always love to sit in this one chair by the window. It is the place that allows me to write, create, and dream. Now I realize it is in the "children's area" of the home. Since your class, I've been able to identify that I feel safe here and able to connect with God in this spot more than any other place in my home."

These are just a few of the empowering statements I get from students and clients. So often we look to friends or a professional to tell us what needs to be done in our own dwellings, when the correct answer is truly within us.

We have been conditioned to go to the expert to find the solution to the problem. But many times the professional doesn't ask the right question, or sometimes they don't hear or understand what is truly being said. We just need guidance and encouragement to ask the right question and then go within and listen for the answer to be given.

Long ago, when we lived in close union with our environment — the land, plants, seasons and animals — we instinctively knew when to do, or not do, something. We would get signs or feelings as to the appropriate action to take at that time. For survival, we had to *trust* in our instincts and intuition, and they became stronger and easier to access. Our instincts were, at this very high level, for our highest and best good.

What we want to do, now, is to create a living environment where we can learn to trust our gut feelings, or intuition, more. One way we can learn to do this is by becoming conscious of the way we feel about things and what we like doing in our space as much as possible.

If you are renting, it may take a bit more ingenuity to accomplish. However, that too has its rewards because you can "practice" and take this experience with you. When you own the property, you do have more flexibility. Easy things like painting one wall or the front door can be completed with a small investment of time and money.

It may benefit you at this time to learn more about Feng Shui methodology. The last quotation I gave in this chapter — the one where the children's area is mentioned — has to do with Feng Shui.

What is Feng Shui?

First let me give you a very short background on Feng Shui and how I got into it.

Thousands of years ago in China they would call on the expertise of a Feng Shui Master to tell the Emperor and very well-to-do people the appropriate location on which to build a home. They believed in many of the sciences which our culture terms the "occult" sciences — like astrology and numerology.

With this information in hand, the Master would scour the countryside to find the right site and then position the building in the correct direction to bring all possible good fortune — health, wealth, power, love, and fame — to this individual.

It was an oral tradition. The Master would closely guard the information so it would not fall into evil hands to be used against his clients or to harm other individuals. He would carefully choose the students with which he would share this knowledge. There would be many rituals and many ceremonies.

One day I went to an interior designers' industry trade show. I attended a workshop on Feng Shui. Some things made sense from a design perspective, but most of it really grated against my Western upbringing and cultural belief systems.

If it hadn't been for a story the lecturer, Professor Lin Yun, shared, that would probably have been the end of my exposure to this ancient philosophy/science/art, but he did share a story which I found to be so unbelievable, I had to find out more.

Therefore, I sat in on another lecture later that same day, only to learn during the course of the lecture there were several problems with my own house which were creating problems in my life. Those were real situations in my life and when I took appropriate action, much to my amazement, those problems did change!

At first, I really didn't believe that Feng Shui had anything to do with the outcomes. I was the true skeptic. However, more and more situations changed from potential "bad Feng Shui" to "good Feng Shui" as I tried them. I studied, questioned, and applied what I was learning for many years. My interest peaked, and I traveled to take classes from other Masters.

Slowly I began to uncover the deeper meaning of this ancient philosophy. I saw the principle was to honor the home as a spiritual connection to the body, mind, and spirit of the individual who lived there. It became clear that Feng Shui has the potential to help a person discover the gifts they were given by a Higher Power and become the bright, shining beacon of light they were meant to be – an empowered human being.

This was a phenomenal discovery for me. It tied into the intrinsic feelings I had about the importance of home. Several other aspects of design and health care began to make sense as well. The picture was becoming very clear, encompassing many areas.

Then, during a move from one house to another, the final door was opened. The key that unlocked it was energy — *the knowledge and discovery that we can use this subtle force that occurs in each home and each room within the home, to develop the type of life we want.*

Feng Shui theory states that there are nine energy areas of life represented in a room and again throughout the overall house. It goes on to state that if a home is balanced, (determining if a home is "balanced" comes later in another section of this book) then the life of the individual also will be balanced. And a balanced life brings all good to it — an attraction of positive energy to the home and to the individual.

Working to balance the energy of your home is a lifelong commitment. **You** are constantly changing and so must your home in order to reflect the "new" you. So much for the idea of designing a home once and never having to touch it again!

Briefly, I will explain the nine areas of the Ba-Gua and some of the meanings for each of those areas:

The nine areas are career, knowledge, family, wealth, fame, partnership, children, helpful people/benefactors, and health. In the questions section, you probably had a thought or pictured something for many of these areas. That's a start.

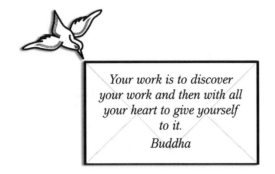

*Your work is to discover
your work and then with all
your heart to give yourself
to it.*
Buddha

Career

We all have careers. For many years the concept of being a homemaker was not thought of as a career, and it most certainly is. It takes time, knowledge, commitment, and energy as do all professions. But we usually think of career as being paid for our efforts — paid in a monetary fashion.

The area of career helps us to put into perspective the meaning of life as well as the quality of life. It is very important to acknowledge and value all jobs and professions, paid or not.

I have a very good friend, Sharon, who did a presentation at a conference for women. At one point she asked for 10 volunteers to come up. Next she gave each of them a piece of cardboard with a title or name on it. They were doctor, lawyer, astronaut, janitor, teacher, president, child, parent, nurse, and volunteer.

She asked them to talk among themselves and come to a conclusion as to an order of importance. Then line up in this order. They had 3 minutes. It was fascinating to watch this process being done.

How would you rate each of these professions? Which one would you say is most important? Why? Which is last? What is the reasoning behind all of your decisions?

I purposely did not tell you more specifically the demographics of the group. Were these women executives? Doctors? Teachers? Lawyers? Housekeepers for a large hotel chain? Mothers? Nurses? Volunteers?

Do you get the picture? We often set the importance of the "label" according to our own perspective. If this were a group of teachers, nine of which were being asked to assume a different identity, how would they feel toward these "new" titles? Would they vote to have their new identity be more important? Would they want the teacher position to still be the most important? Or would they be objective, prioritizing the different positions according to general consensus of the 10 people involved?

When the time was up, the audience was to agree or disagree and tell why they made that decision. A discussion ensued. Can you see that depending upon how a person feels about themselves, at that point in their life, their perspective of the importance of each "title" will vary? If you were just promoted or laid-off, can you see how that would influence your thinking?

Sharon had done this presentation with different groups many times, mostly entrepreneurs who had been in a variety of careers. Usually the high-paid professional or high-powered positions were rated as the most important, with the roles of child, janitor and teacher ranked in a lesser role. Their placements were quite different than today.

The above group of women had been invited by the Soroptimist for "A Day for Women". A majority of women in this audience were now full-time mothers in a community with high values and appreciation of family life. More than half of them had been in a "professional position" for several years and had chosen to leave their professions in order to spend quality time raising families. They would probably return to the "work force" later, but priorities had changed for them.

This was reflected in the choices made by the original 10 volunteers as well as the audience. Child, parent, teacher, and janitor were voted among the top four by both volunteers and audience (slightly different positioning by the two). The last in the list also varied, but they were lawyer, president, and astronaut.

As you might guess there are several reasons I share this story. The two most important are: 1) to give value to all careers, and, 2) to realize how much importance we put in titles or labels as to a person's worth.

The area of career is the part of our life that we give value to in the form of time. Maybe it's a job or maybe it is raising a family. It is how we spend 8, 10, possibly even 12 hours or more per day. Or it could be a combination of choices we make.

If you are working part-time at one job and part-time at another, those relate to career. Going to school and working would relate to career. Parenting and working are careers. Any combination of time spent toward the improvement of the quality of life for yourself and other individuals would be considered **an act of career**.

All the jobs you have ever done are part of your career. For those of us who have had 40, 50 or more jobs, it has been a process for us to learn where our talents lie, what is natural for us, what makes our heart sing.

Career is: our "calling" in life or "life purpose," the "follow your bliss" concept, and often "the road less traveled".

Is career represented in your home environment? Is it represented by piles of paper and a brief case? Or do you have items you have created visible for yourself and others to view?

Are there awards? Anything symbolic of your work? Maybe pictures or artifacts of places you have traveled through your profession?

If your career is focused on life in the home, then do you have special, even sacred, artifacts displayed which represent your "career"? Are there crayon drawings, snapshots, and example of hobbies around the house?

Career is important and needs to be expressed. What about the energy of career is calling to you? How might you acknowledge it?

*I hear and I forget. I see and
I remember. I do and I
understand.*
Chinese Proverb

Knowledge

As human beings, we have the ability to learn — to gain knowledge about the world around us. We learn from teachers, books, and computers. We have on-the-job training, and our employers send us for training. The seminar and workshop industry are booming businesses.

We also learn from life experiences, ours and others. In fact several organizations are set up just to that end, where they teach OPE — Other People's Experiences.

We live in the Information Age. In fact, we are over-whelmed with information. We receive more mail in a day than our parents did in a week. And we may do most of our communication by phone, fax, or e-mail.

For the first time in history, we can "see history" in the making. Technology has given us television and satellites which, in turn, gives us instantaneous connection to people and events around the world.

We strive for higher education and degrees, and while they are important, we find ourselves often valuing those aspects of learning above other forms. I suggest here, there are other types of learning or knowledge that we could also honor.

Recently, I was privileged to be asked to participate in the Opening Prayer Ceremony at an Esalen Indian Pow-Wow. It was an incredible experience for the body, mind and spirit. During one part, the Chief was talking about the traditions of his people, and how they "knew" if someone was ill even when they were not physically in the same place with them.

They knew what "healthy" energy for that person felt like, and even though they were not next to them, could sense "unhealthy, or not normal," energy emanating from them. He went on to say that they would also "know" when someone was thinking of them, what we call telepathy. In order to locate food and water for survival, they "knew" when an animal was close by and where to find shallow underground streams.

Today some Indian tribes prohibit telephones, televisions, and other technologies on their land in order to keep these intrusions from interfering with the Great Spirits gift of "inner knowing".

Having experiences in life is a type of knowledge, and what you do with that experience is another learning process. When we have a "gut feeling", or use our intuition, that becomes part of the learning process as we start to trust those feelings. We learn such feelings are warranted and valuable.

Our Western mentality takes education for granted, expecting it as a "gift". Sometimes, it's the best education money can buy, yet often it is not valued. I am sure you know someone who had the financial ability to go to a leading university, attended it, and abused the privilege. It just might be that attending an educational institution for that individual is inappropriate. Their talents may be in a different area. Not everyone excels in the classroom environment or wants to. They may be very aware of the external environment – the land, trees, and animals. They may instinctively be able to diagnose the problem with an animal who is sick or a plant that is dying. They have the gift of deep inner knowing.

In this area of knowledge we are talking about the gathering of knowledge by whatever means there is. Knowledge, as with all aspects of life, is not just about "give me! give me! give me!" or "get! get! get!" It is the dissemination of knowledge as well.

How do we release the knowledge we have? Do we read stories to children? Teach classes or give workshops through schools and organizations? Or participate in active listening, encouraging ideas to explore or thoughts to ponder?

Knowledge has far reaching implications. When we didn't have a means to keep our knowledge alive other than stories or oral traditions, with only stone tablets or limited hand-written manuscripts, no photographs, no tapes (audio or video), and no computers with their CD's and discs, we were constantly "reinventing the wheel" so to speak. Only the most valuable information, that which was needed every day to stay alive, was transmitted. And since we didn't have the ability to communicate quickly between tribes nor townships, much less continents, we lost information and the ability to compare and compile.

Knowledge is to be gathered and shared. It's learning the lessons of life and the consequences we may have to pay for choices we make. It's realizing that our knowledge is a part of a larger consciousness, to be shared with people who will use it for good and value it.

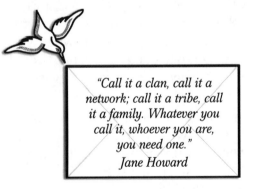

"Call it a clan, call it a network; call it a tribe, call it a family. Whatever you call it, whoever you are, you need one."
Jane Howard

Family

What does family mean to you? Is it your blood relatives? Are they people you live with? Step-mother? In-laws? The term "family" encompasses all of these and many more.

They are people we love to be with, who have a common bond to us. We may love to do the same things. Therefore, we join a club or organization which is designed to enhance that part of our lives through activities built around that common thread.

They may be our parents, grandparents, great-grandparents, and so on. Our children are part of our family and they also have their own area of the Ba-Gua. We will address them later.

It's our ancestors, the heritage we carry with us, our cultural ties. What cultures do our ancestors come from? What religious background did they have and you have growing up? Were some raised in the United States or on another continent? In the city or the country?

How did we play as children? By ourselves? With siblings? In groups? Were we athletic? A bookworm?

What was our past like? Was "family" fun? Constantly moving because a parent was in the service? Adventurous?

The groups you belong to, do they support you? Help you grow? Challenge you to "be all that you can be"? Give you unconditional love? Share experiences, stories, hopes, and dreams? Comfort you when you're down or need a helping hand? Are they "there for you" even when you don't know you need them? Do they gently point out your shortcomings, possibly (but not always) giving you suggestions on ways to improve?

These are some of the qualities of family. Family is a fundamental part of who we are. We draw upon the energy of family many times without realizing it. Many times, people don't survive in this world because "family" was not a strong, healthy entity in their life.

It is history — *your history.* You are a combination of all these parts of family. It's ever changing, expanding and, encompassing more, and more. From the microcosm to the macrocosm, we are the family of Man. And the planet we live on — Earth — is our home.

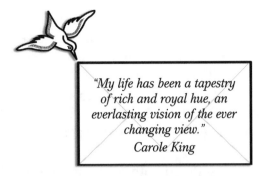

*"My life has been a tapestry
of rich and royal hue, an
everlasting vision of the ever
changing view."*
Carole King

Wealth

Our society is fixated on the importance of money, and while it is important for many reasons, it is not the end all to our existence. But it almost seems to be.

We need money to live. Food, shelter, clothing, and entertainment is exchanged for it. However, ads on billboards, in print, and throughout the media purport the necessity of more and better objects to make us feel fulfilled.

I heard a statement which made me disgusted when I heard it. It was a statistic on the number of hours a young person, by the time they reach the age of 17 years, will have spent with parents, in school, and watching TV or being influenced by the media. It was mind boggling. Quality time with parents – 2,000 hours. Time in school – 20,000 hours. "Influenced by the media" time – 40,000 hours. This was several years ago.

What is time worth? What is the life of a child worth? What value are we putting on the quality of a young person's life, or on any life for that matter?

As I said, we need money for our economy. There has always been a form of exchange – a means to trade for services we don't or can't do, and products we need and do not make ourselves. I think it must have been much simpler in the early days of this world when there were fewer temptations.

The principles and laws around money are still the same. This is not a book on how to gain prosperity. It is a section to help us put the concept of money into a proper perspective. This section is on wealth, i.e. prosperity.

What is wealth? A friend of mine shares a story of a woman who will give you *ONE MILLION DOLLARS!!!* All you need to do is give her your eyes so she might see again. Would you do it?

Anyone who has suffered with a serious illness will tell you they'd give any amount of money to be well. Even a sore throat makes me want to spend the money to be rid of it quickly!

So, is it money we want, or what it can buy? If it's what we can buy, then what do you value most? Objects? Health? Peace of mind? Realized dreams? Retirement in a life-style similar to one you are now living, or better?

Then how do you acquire those things? By learning the *laws of prosperity.* By showing responsible spending. By having a sense of abundance. It's writing down each day the things you are grateful for, and taking care of your health, showing your family your love, and valuing them by spending time with them, praising them, and loving them unconditionally. Circulate and move the energy from lack to abundance. Express abundance by being generous with all your heart. Give, give, give. Your time, your money, yourself, and your love.

That's one of the laws of prosperity — to circulate it — not hoard or throw it away, but allow it to flow in a responsible manner. It's one of our greatest challenges as a nation, learning to spend in accordance with our income.

There is a class I took many years ago called the 4T Prosperity Class. In this class I discovered what each of those Ts stood for — Tithing of Time, Talents, and Treasures (money). I was amazed by the shift in consciousness that occurred around not only money, but also the value of my time and how many talents I have. I also learned that tithing usually means giving 10% of your assets to whatever feeds you spiritually each week.

By going through the process, my life began to feel richer. At that particular time for me the flow of money into my life was like a dry riverbed during a drought – nothing there! By the end of the eight weeks, it was a small creek which has improved and enlarged ever since.

What do you tithe? Is it 10%? Do you do it each week or once a month? Do you only give from one of the T's? Just your talents, or your money? Not your time? Or do you give only money, rarely giving your time or talents.

When you discover the *REAL RICHES* in life, you become a *VERY WEALTHY PERSON.*

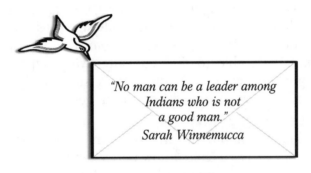

"No man can be a leader among Indians who is not a good man."
Sarah Winnemucca

Fame

What do you think about when you hear the word "fame"? Most people think of someone being well-known, popular, and while this is part of it, it is a very small part. Fame has to do with the very essence of you – who you are, your beliefs, values and integrity.

For years I accepted who I thought I was – a very friendly child who loved sports. I lived across the street from a school, and every afternoon when classes were finished, all holidays, and during the summer, I would play there. I became very involved in the Girl's Athletic League and ran for Commissioner of Girls as soon as I was old enough. I was devastated when I lost the first time, but I decided to try again.

My uncle was great at drawing cartoons, so he helped me with my "campaign posters." The next time, I won. It felt really great and everyone knew me. But then I went to high school.

The high school brought together nine elementary schools, so only 1/9 the population knew me. I found out it wasn't really "cool" to be active in sports, that beauty wins, and I was very much over weight.

To add to that deflated self-esteem, the first boy I ever dated dropped me because I won a swim meet. He was not athletic and it hurt his ego. So I started to change who I was in order to have friends. Sound familiar?

I heard some astounding statistics just last week about girls ages 9-14 years. During that age bracket, Caucasian girl's self-esteem will drop 32%, Latino girl's self-esteem will drop 38%, and African-American girl's self-esteem will drop only 6%. I haven't been able to find out why two groups are so high a percentage while another is so low. But I would imagine it has to do with cultural perspectives of womanhood and beauty.

It has taken a long time for me to become reacquainted with the person I was as a child. I now understand that it took a *total* loss of identity, having no self-esteem, before I realized it was gone. A little bite here, another there. A loss in beliefs, values, and trust.

At that point, I felt I had no reason to live. It took a life-changing experience to help me regain my true identity, and later, to understand the major role this area (Fame) of the Ba-Gua played in my life. That's a great story and another book.

The area of Fame represents the values of "Do unto others as you would have them do unto you." It's the area of truth, justice, laws — laws pertaining to the legal system and laws pertaining to the spiritual system. It is the area that connects the *riches of life* (Wealth) with *relationships* (Partnership). It's the intimate look at one's self — "In-to-me-see, intimacy."

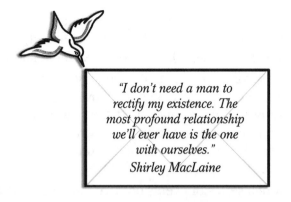

"I don't need a man to rectify my existence. The most profound relationship we'll ever have is the one with ourselves."
Shirley MacLaine

Partnership

Ah, the Marriage Corner! This has been an area of "trial and error" in my life. However, I say this with a sense of joy and wonder as I have really learned what it takes to have this area be in harmony with all the rest. This is not only within my own relationships, but within the relationships of my many clients throughout the years.

It is sometimes said that we teach what we most need to learn. Imagine for a moment, how I feel when I walk into a person's life and the outcome they want is the same thing I want? This is very often the case, for what better way to see what I must do than to see it reflected in another person's life? It is truly difficult to evaluate our own lives and surroundings objectively.

And as challenges go, I have had so many insights into the magnitude of this area that it deserves a book unto itself. But for now, let me give you a few of the key issues.

Partnership — the one-on-one relationship with another individual. How does one merge with another without losing one's own identity? This has been a question that has been asked for centuries and will probably continue to puzzle people for many more.

It helps to know what the qualities are you want in a partner. I'm certain there are physical qualities, but for now let's reduce the number by focusing on a few key words. In a relationship you probably would like some or all of these — devoted, loving, faithful (filled with faith), constant, loyal, covenant (promise or agreement), unity (oneness), and harmony.

Read those words again, carefully! Do they stir your soul? Take each word and repeat it over and over, gently, with reverence. Do any feel more important that the other? Are you filled with emotions, images from the past, and/or feelings with any of them? Write your own definition of each word. Add that paper to this section.

It wasn't until a series of events occurred in my life which led me to discover my own spirituality that I came to have a passionate connection with these words. For you see, it is impossible for you to understand, or to integrate, the highest meaning of these words until you discover your connection to a Higher Power, the Divine, Great Creator, or God — whatever the name of the "Being of Highest Good" is for you.

Therein lies the challenge for most people in this area of balance of the Ba-Gua in their life. We think we understand something, perhaps another person's pain or heartache, but until you have walked in the other's shoes, you can only guess what they are feeling. So, how can you find your soul mate, if you haven't experienced these qualities of the Divine? If you have not experienced them, how will you recognize them in another? It's a journey. A journey of discovery, realization and learning.

The area of partnership is an area of relationship building — the building of a relationship to the Higher Power in each of us, a connection to our *SOUL*. The connection can be 1) *OUR* relationship to God/Higher Power, 2) our relationship to a spouse/significant other, and 3) our business one-on-one relationships.

All will have a soul connection requiring much nurturing. This nurturing will command our attention to the qualities I listed earlier within ourselves — devoted, loving, faithful (filled with faith), constant, loyal, covenant (promise or agreement), unity (oneness), and harmony — in order to be able to produce the quality we want in our other relationships.

As I said in the beginning of this partnership section, this has been an area of trial and error in my life, and I say with a great deal of joy, wonder, and gratitude, it has been a glorious journey that I've shared with many kindred spirits which has brought this area into harmony with all the rest of the areas of my life. If you nurture this area, you too, will receive the blessings of those qualities which, in turn, will bring joy into your life.

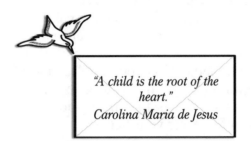

"A child is the root of the heart."
Carolina Maria de Jesus

Children

"to be as little children"

Many years ago I did a presentation to a group of married couples who had made the decision to be childless. When I came to this area of the Ba-Gua, their comments were "We can skip this area. We don't want children." Nothing could have been further from the truth since most of these people were highly sensitive individuals. The children's area of the Ba-Gua is just as important as all the others, no matter what decision has been made about having or not having children, for it is the area of childlike qualities.

What do you think of when you hear the word "children?" Do you think of holding a child? Is the child crying or smiling? Is the child running and playing? Are they lying on the ground while looking at a ladybug on a blade of grass or wishing upon a shooting star?

All these are qualities of this area of children. This is the area to be a child – to nurture the child within, play, wonder, and dream. When you have children, and you make quality time to be with them, both you and your child benefit because the "little kid" within you comes out to play. There is fun, frolicking, and fantasy to be had.

What does it take to be a child? Where would you go? What would you do? What colors would you wear? How would you fix your hair? Would you even worry about your hair? Do you have a cat, dog, canary, fish, hamster, snake, monkey, rabbit, pig, or toad for a pet? Do you like to play with dolls or cars? Are books your companion? Is there "an imaginary friend" who plays with you? Is there a toy that makes you smile or a dog that makes you laugh? Do you play "tea party" or "Star Wars"? Does Mom rock you in her arms in a rocking chair? Does grandma make cookies for you or does she design a beautiful quilt comforter for your bed?

These are the energies of children – to be carefree, child-like, playful, nurtured, loved, creative, fanciful, joyful, emotional, inquisitive, mischievous, wishful, hopeful, trusting, youthful, adventuresome, smart, foolish, natural and to connect with nature.

Children know what to do, when to do it, and how to do it! When young they are not afraid, they take risks. They know they will be taken care of, protected, held, loved. How does your inner child feel about this? Does it sound scary or fun?

We want to have fun in our lives. We want to be artistic and creative. Creativity is a very positive force. It is the area for creative endeavors as well as procreation. Both of them have gestation periods, birthing process, youthful exuberance, adolescent rebellion, adult responsibility, mid-life transformation, and maturing reality along with wisdom.

So what is it about the children's area that called to you? This is a very strong intuitive area. Have you been nurturing the inner child and your intuition? Can you "come out and play" for a while? Decide to play with this area and you'll bring a playfulness to all areas of your life. It lightens up the more serious times bringing laughter to you which, in turn, is both very creative and very healing. To find out more about this area, go sit with your children or someone else's children, or find a place in your mind for your child within to be a kid. Have you gone to a toy store recently to find something just for you? Have you played "dress-up" or baseball within the last few months?

Last Christmas, I went to San Francisco with a soon-to-be first-time mother and three teenager girls who attend an alternative high school. Often when I go to "The City" it's usually dressed as an interior designer to tour the showrooms for clients or I can also go in my jeans to be just one of the people from the neighborhood. This time, this experience was to let my little kid in me out to play, to go to the department stores, try on clothes that we could not afford just to get the feel of it, to go to FAO Schwartz to dance on and play the big piano with our feet, and to go to the Sheraton Palace to have "High Tea" at 4:00 in the afternoon.

Later, when I returned home, I found it much easier to decorate and rearrange the house for Christmas. My creative, Christmas-loving kid inside helped me. The spirit of the little child stayed with me, creating joy and laughter easily. When you are good to the playful child within, joy and fun are abundant. This is the children's area of your home.

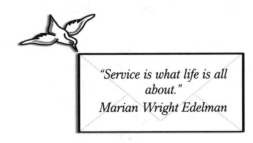

"*Service is what life is all about.*"
Marian Wright Edelman

Helpful People

Have you ever been alone, totally isolated from other individuals? Have you ever lived by yourself without family or friends geographically close to you? Can you imagine how you might feel if you were seriously ill with no one around to help you?

When I talk to single groups or with my single clients, the biggest fear most of them have is the fear of being sick without someone to care for them. What if you could not get out of bed to fix food for yourself? What if you fell and could not get to a phone? What if there was a catastrophe at your isolated dwelling, would anyone know to come and help you?

These are situations you probably will not experience since we have the world of technology with cellular phones and monitoring devices, but for hundreds of years it was a major concern. An isolated person might die from the elements. An elderly person might fall and not be found for days.

What other ways do people help you? Do you grow your own vegetables and hunt for wildlife to feed you and your family? Did you build the building you live in all by yourself? When your child had a cough and sore throat last winter, did you fix a cure for it yourself by finding herbs, honey or other ingredients and mixing them together in the proper portions to heal them? Probably not.

We rely on other people to help us through our daily lives all the time yet may not acknowledge them. The taxi or bus driver, the bagger at the supermarket, the dry cleaners, our mentor, partner, best friend. Everyone we meet is a helpful person in our lives, we just don't always perceive it at the time.

Have you ever been thinking about someone only to run into them an hour or a day later? I often thought I was the only one who benefited from the "chance meeting" until I started to pay attention, to listen more closely, to the statements they made when we met.

I would hear things like, "I was just thinking of you earlier this morning," or, "We were just discussing Feng Shui last night and I thought of you," or, "Come to think about it, I need the name of that friend of yours you told me about last year who does gardening because my gardener just quit." These are ways we help other people.

This area is sometimes called the "benefactor" area. It benefits people. How are we taught to sell? Find out what the person wants and sell them on the "benefits" that address those issues. So our lives revolve around benefiting or helping other people. I believe we have been put here to give of ourselves to our fellow man, to serve.

One of the other aspects of this particular corner of the Ba-Gua is its impact on traveling. If you like to travel, this area is filled with potential; add maps and books on places of interest to you. If you travel with your work and would like to spend more time at home, you will want to modify the energy in this space. Several of my clients have had this situation. With one, we changed the color of the room to yellow, to "ground" or stabilize the area. With the other, we moved a piece of furniture that was at an angle and placed it flat against the wall, again to stabilize the energy.

Traveling has to do with the fact that we are part of the earth ecosystem. We may need to travel to locate a suitable place to live where we can survive the climate and find food and water.

Many cultures are aware and respectful of the ecosystem, recognizing the interconnectedness of all creatures and the need for balance within the systems. When the food chain is altered for whatever reason, the animals will either travel to find a new food source or die. Since we are part of the food chain, we, too, must travel to maintain suitable food sources. This travel may take us to other planets or to the depths of the sea.

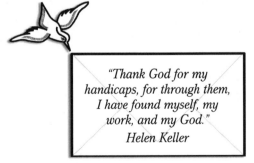

"Thank God for my handicaps, for through them, I have found myself, my work, and my God."
Helen Keller

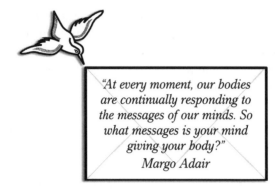

"At every moment, our bodies are continually responding to the messages of our minds. So what messages is your mind giving your body?"
Margo Adair

Health

The first thing most of us think about when the word health is mentioned, is our physical health. We may think of low-fat, high carbs, the food groups, fresh foods, herbs, vegetarian, etc. We might think of young body builders, organized exercise programs, walking, biking, kayaking, golf or tennis. These are important parts of being healthy.

When I was growing up, the focus was mostly on our nutritional health, and yet knowledge about nutrition at that time was very limited. The role physical exercise played in our well-being was almost nonexistent. Thank goodness, since then, there have been many new discoveries, and as science, technology, religions and cultures blend their knowledge, we will advance even more.

One of the more recent discoveries has been the role our mind plays in our health. There are even organizations, like the Ozark Research Institute, where they are documenting the results of the "power of the mind," and its effect on healing. Many places do biofeedback to help reduce stress in the physical body.

The role our home plays in our health is dynamic. We have physical, mental, emotional and spiritual bodies, and each one is probably just as complex as our physical body, which we are still learning about. They each have a relationship to the other. They also have a relationship to their surroundings.

Just as the physical body is affected by an improperly designed chair, so can a mental and emotional body be affected by an improperly placed picture or piece of furniture. There is a constant interaction among all of them that affects each one of them.

As you will learn in greater detail when you discover how to use the Ba-Gua, the area of health is located in the center of our house so it touches all areas of our lives. Of course we know that our physical health will affect our outlook on life, why wouldn't all other areas of health – mental, emotional and spiritual – also affect it?

Every one of these areas of the Ba-Gua, representing corresponding areas of our lives, is a part of our whole life. But is it an active part of our life? Have we forgotten some of them? Are some far more important to us than others?

There needs to be a balance in our life. These nine areas that encompass all aspects of us need equal attention. However, it might be that we need to focus intently on one of them at a time for a while. Then, as the one is reduced, the focus might need to be redirected to another one, bringing it to the center of our attention.

The ancients of many cultures understood the impact our environment has on the human psyche, that creating a beautiful and functional home is only part of the whole concept. A home is a place to nurture and rejuvenate the vital force that lives within us. It is a metaphor of us as human beings and symbolic of how we are living our lives. The home is sacred space and a major influence in our lives, creating a place with space to help us be more productive from a spiritual point of view.

There is power in this place we call home – a sacredness unlike any other in our lives. We create it in our own image. It is a reflection of who we are and what we dream.

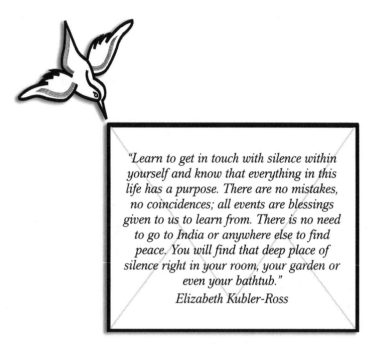

"Learn to get in touch with silence within yourself and know that everything in this life has a purpose. There are no mistakes, no coincidences; all events are blessings given to us to learn from. There is no need to go to India or anywhere else to find peace. You will find that deep place of silence right in your room, your garden or even your bathtub."

Elizabeth Kubler-Ross

Floor Plans/Space Planning

> "The point of nonviolence is to build a floor, a strong new floor, beneath which we can no longer sink."
> Joan Baez

When designing our home space, one of the first things we need to do is to become familiar with the layout of the house. This is called making a floor plan of the room or house. When you look at model homes or go to rent an apartment, you often are given a drawing of the space which shows where the doors, windows and rooms are located. We are going to do this for your dwelling.

If you are planning to work with one room, you only need to do that one room. But if the plan entails more than one room, it might benefit you to do the whole house. Sometimes when you are looking at the floor plan of the whole area you have to work with, you discover there are small spaces that might be just the right size to fill a need, like a closet that can be a computer workspace or an alcove to fit a TV so it doesn't protrude into the room.

This plan will serve several purposes. One is to help us plan space for the functions that will happen in each room, Another will be to see what the flow of traffic is (the Feng Shui term would be "chi"). A third will be to help us place the Ba-Gua which will help us find the best possible positions for sitting, beds and desks.

The tools you need to do this include a measuring device (probably a 25' to 100' metal tape since it won't distort the measurements when it is pulled taut), masking tape or something to make marks on the floor without leaving permanent marks on it or carpeting, a large pad of paper with cardboard backing (legal or grid), and pencils with erasers to draw a rough sketch of the shape of the dwelling or room and to list the measurements.

I have found it easiest for me to put these distances in feet and inches rather than all inches. This also helps if you will be using one of the boxed floor plan kits available at many home improvement centers. These planning kits contain most items you will be needing; scaled ruler, 1/4" grid cardboard layout surface with peel-and-stick symbols, including walls, windows, doors, furniture, cabinets, bathroom fixtures, kitchen fixtures and plants.

First we need to sketch the shape of the house. We can do this by walking around the exterior of the building, if it is a free standing building. If it is not, we work from the inside, drawing one room at a time and taking all the interior wall measurements plus the addition of space for the studs and wallboard. You only need to measure to the nearest inch. Be sure to label which floor you are on if there is more than one story you are working with.

We need to measure the width of doors and windows and show which way they move (doors are hinged on one side, windows may be double-hung, slide one direction, or open inward or outward), any moldings that will affect the placement of furniture, architectural features like furnaces, fireplaces, closets, counters, fixed bookcases, elevators, radiators, stairwells, etc. We might also need the measurements from the floor to the bottom of the window sills and overall height of the doors and ceilings if possible. Be sure to double check your measurements or better still have someone else retrace your work to be certain you haven't transposed a number or made a mistake.

Depending on what amount of work you will be doing, we may need to know which walls are load bearing. But for now we will assume this is more a decorating project than a remodel. We do need to know where the plumbing is located within the bathrooms and kitchen as well as any other water features you might have in the space.

Now we need to put it on the grid board or draw it on grid paper. It usually is best to use a 1/4" scale equals 1'. This keeps the plan at a manageable size. If you need to be more accurate with the detail of size, you may want to have the scale be 1/2" equals 1' or maybe even 1" equals 1.' It's harder to get a complete house plan on a reasonable size sheet of paper, so I might do a house in 1/4" scale and then with the rooms where I needed more detail, I'd switch to 1" to 1'. The professional scale rulers have many ratios available while the ones that come in the pre-boxed plan kits usually only have 1/4" scale rulers.

Place the sheet of paper or the grid board so the widest part of the house will fit the longest side of the paper or board. It helps if this long edge is facing you, then you don't have to reach as far, and having a table where this project may rest undisturbed is very beneficial.

For most people it works best to start in the upper left hand corner because that is the way we have been taught to read, but if you have been raised in a different culture, pick the area that works best for you. There is no "right way" to this part of the project. Don't be surprised if you have to erase a few times, or start over. Unless you are accustomed to doing this, it can be challenging to a novice. Stay with it. It doesn't have to be a work of art.

Starting at a corner, measure each wall and draw a line using the scaled ruler. If the building you are working with is a perfect square or rectangle, draw one complete line for the exterior of the building, then mark off each room measurement along the line. If the building is irregular in shape, you will want to do one room at a time.

Now we need to mark the interior walls. It always pays to double check your measurements. You will probably know when you have made a mistake when the exterior measurements and interior walls will do not match; however, once in a while a couple of errors happen that make it look right. If it's only a few inches you can adjust each room a little.

After you have drawn the walls in the room, locate all the doors and windows. We need to know which side of the door(s) has the hinge. If the door is a pocket door or just an opening with no door, we need to know that also. Windows can open inward or outward as well as slide, so we need to know not only where on the wall they are located, but also whether they swing into the room. These measurements would often be part of what we call an elevation of the wall, but at this time we are only going to do the floor plan. We just need to know if the window will affect the placement of a piece of furniture.

We're now ready to put in some of the architectural features. Your space may not have some of these because it is part of a larger complex. But if these features are located where they touch any part of your interior or exterior walls, including a garage, please make a note of them at this time.

We want to know about; fireplaces, furnaces, hot water heaters, washer/dryer areas, wash basins, elevators, stairwells, dumb waiters, flues/vents/shafts in or around your space, bath tubs, showers, sinks, toilets, bidets, saunas, hot tubs (inside or on decks), dishwashers, stove, oven, refrigerator, separate freezer, bar sinks, indoor bar-be-ques, atriums, skylights, and fountains.

Since we are going to be using this floor plan for many different aspects – function and space planning, location of the Ba-Gua, possible remodeling or creation of specialized interior and exterior spaces – it would be advantageous to make several photo copies at this time.

You might want to get one that is smaller than the original if you think you might need to fax a copy to someone. I also like to have several enlargements made, especially of each room, as it is easier to work with minute details when the scale is 1/2" to 1' or larger. If you are working with a planning kit you may not want to make them larger as the pieces of furniture will be made for your 1/4" scale drawing and will not work on a 1/2" drawing unless you enlarge the furniture cutouts at the same time you enlarge the floor plan.

Space Planning

The art of space planning could be another whole book unto itself; however, we need to know what you have in the way of furniture, how much space you have in which to put the furniture, and what functions will happen in this room.

As I shared with you in one of my earlier stories about a client, sometimes you can't do all the functions you want in a room or you can't put in all the furniture. Then we need to set priorities. Do we want to have a permanent game table to be able to work on puzzles or do we need a multipurpose flat surface that can be used for school projects, sewing, or family dining? This is where we need to "get real," so please write down the answers to the questions. It will help you to be more conscious of your environment and have realistic expectations, relieving some of the anxiety around your planning.

Who lives in the home? Only adults? How many? What ages? How many children? What are their ages? Very young? Teenagers? Do you each have your own bedroom? Who shares? Does the sharing work?

It is very important to look at these questions on a regular basis. Sometimes we have two children together in a room, one boy and one girl, because they are both young. Now they have grown, so you may decide it would be better to have two sisters or two brothers with a wider age disparity sharing a room. This may seem obvious to you, but you would be surprised how often our lives keep us so busy we forget to look at and do the obvious. This could also apply to a husband and wife. They may need separate bedrooms to get the rest they need because of work patterns or health challenges.

What are the daily activities performed by each person? Is it the same each day or does it change? Is it the same for weekdays and different for weekends? Definitely look at the activities for one week and maybe even for a month.

I have one friend who writes a newsletter for a club. Hence, her activity needs change one week of the month. You might be surprised at the number of activities that occur regularly during one time of the year and not another, so think about and write down the things you do during the different seasons. Also your needs change as the children grow, you get new pets, and we get older. Function follows need.

How do you use the rooms now? Write down each room and include a list of the activities done in each. Do you have a student who needs quiet in order to study while another person might be using the space to watch TV? If that were the case, you might want to make a place in the student's room for studying, or devote a spare bedroom to study and meditative activities.

Maybe you need the "great room" type of arrangement when everyone likes to spend time together. There can be people in the kitchen, some watching TV, others doing hobbies or puzzles and still have room for the toddlers to romp and play.

If you already have a workable plan, great! If you don't, how could it be changed?

Before you decide to move or remodel, since some of us cannot afford to do either, list the things that are working for you in each room. Do the rooms serve you well except for one part of your life? Could you move the furniture you have around in order to make it work? Could you take a desk from the office and move it to the "great room?" Maybe the small table by the sofa could be used as a desk or flat surface in the bedroom so you can pay the family bills?

If the room works on most levels, but you need another piece of furniture, is it something you can afford right now? Is it something you need to have custom-built? Sometimes you can sell a couple of pieces that don't work for you and use the money received from those to purchase or custom-build a piece. That will solve several problems.

Many of my clients have solved their problems this way. Now, in many large metropolitan areas, there are consignment shops where you can display your furniture or look for used furniture to fit your changing life-styles. With so many people moving, combining households, dissolving relationships, and having roommates, along with supplies, items used for short periods of time in the "staging" of homes for sale, the options are numerous. You can buy or sell furniture, rugs, accessories, cabinets, architectural detailing, kitchen and bathroom fixtures in these places, at garage sales, or through newspaper ads.

What about the traffic flow within each room and between rooms with related activities? Is it easy to walk around the room? Does the door open all the way or is it partially blocked? Is the laundry area close to the bedrooms? The dining room adjoining the kitchen?

Again, these are things that would be nice to have if you are planning to remodel, but if you can't because you're renting or the cost of remodeling isn't in the budget until the kids graduate from college, is there something you could do or find in the way of a piece of furniture that would make your life work better for you?

Could you remove a wash basin in the laundry room and replace it with a wall mounted, fold-down table where you could fold clothes? Would that help? It would if you wouldn't have to carry the clothes in a laundry basket to the other end of the house. Then each member of the family could take their own items to their rooms and put them away.

Would a baker's rack in the eating nook give you extra storage for baskets and large bowls so they no longer gather on the floor or take up prime kitchen space in the cabinets or on top of the counter?

It would probably be a good idea to talk with other members of the family to gather their input. Sometimes one person has a feeling about how things should be which has never been discussed.

Once I went to rearrange some things in the kitchen when my daughter came home and told me she really didn't like it that way. It really didn't matter to me, but it did to her. She had recently had knee surgery which made it difficult for her to bend over to reach a pan she used almost every day.

Communication is one of the biggest challenges we face in our society. We do not ask people what they think or how something will impact their lives before we do it. Here is an opportunity to practice this lost art form. There will be compromises made in the course of this process; but at least everyone old enough to have an opinion, or knowledgeable about the situation, can have a say in it. Often great ideas come from these discussions because of the brainstorming that occurs. This also makes each member of the family feel important, as though they truly are "part of the family."

First, we need to arrange the furniture you have so it serves you functionally. Most of the time the sofa will go in the living area and the bed in the bedroom. But if you need an extra bed for an aging parent and there is no place else in the house to put it, you just might have to place that bed in the living room.

How are you going to give them privacy while allowing others to watch TV? I'll suggest right now the use of screens, room dividers, large pieces of furniture and plants since this may not be a question that comes up again. Also, make certain anything heavy that is placed in the center of the room is far enough away from an elderly person in bed, bolted down or held in place with brackets. This is not just in earthquake country; someone leaning against the furniture might push it off balance.

There would be other considerations as well having a bed in the living room. How do you make it quiet for them when they want to sleep or the level of noise or activity from children is annoying? You may need a second area for TV watching such as a study or den. You may not be thinking of these things right now, but with an aging population and rising medical and housing costs, this may soon be a reality for you. The "baby boomers" are also known as the "sandwich generation" because our adult children are living with us as are our aging parents.

From a design perspective it is nice to have a focal point in the room. It might be a window-with-a-view, fireplace, entertainment center, or artwork. Often you will have several focal points in a room due to architectural features and furniture groupings.

Furniture groupings in the living and family rooms are usually created to contain certain activities. There may be a place to watch TV, another to have a conversation among friends, and still a third for a more intimate one-on-one conversation or to sit reading a book quietly by yourself or with your loved one close by.

Bedrooms often have many functions as well. It's nice to have a dresser, chest, armoire and night stands if you have the space for them. Besides sleeping, you may need a desk to do school work, pay household bills, write letters, or check your e-mail. Maybe an altar or meditation area is wanted. A cozy chair away from other people in the house might be calling to you.

When placing your furniture cutouts on your grid plan, here are a few guidelines for you to consider:

*   *Leave 3 feet between furniture pieces to allow people to walk. A person can get through smaller areas but they feel uncomfortable. If there is someone using a wheel chair they will need that much room to get through also.*
*   *You need 3 feet around the edges of your eating nook/ dining room tables for people to easily get up from a chair without hitting a wall or another piece of furniture.*
*   *The best distance from a sofa to a coffee table is about 15."*
*   *It's nice to have 24"-30" between the bed and any other furniture or wall with 36" or more preferable at the foot of the bed.*

When you have finished placing the furniture cutouts on your plan, go through the list of activities you have for each person. Have you created a space for each one? Do all the areas work from a functional perspective? Does each person have their own "private" space?

If all the needs and wants of the family are met, congratulations! If not, leave the plan alone for a few days, then revisit it. Your subconscious mind will be working to help you figure out alternatives to the problems. Go back to it over a period of weeks if possible. Ask friends, or take it to an home improvement center to see if they can help you with ideas. This is the mental/logical part to designing your home space.

In the meantime, we can move to the next level of awareness about your home . . . the Ba-Gua. It will give you more ideas for your subconscious to play with and to stimulate it. For the Ba-Gua will give you insights as to the location of energies within your home and your life. It may help you decide where to put the desk in a room or which of the spare bedrooms would make the best study or play room. It may also help you decide if some ideas you had really are the ones for you or not. Or just the opposite, it may create such strong emotional feelings about a place within your home that you change a proposed location for a new one.

The Ba-Gua

At this point I need to share with you more information on the history of Feng Shui and my experiences with it. As I explained earlier, this was a philosophy I was very uncomfortable with. If it hadn't been for the story Professor Lin Yun shared in the class that day, I am certain I would not be here today writing this book.

This story was so unbelievable and horrifying, bringing up a Pandora's Box of desperation and emotions, that I had trouble with Feng Shui and the way I was designing homes for many years. I choose not to share this story, in written form, for a very good reason.

There is something about the way we, as human beings, believe – to the extreme – in the written word. If the words are positive, the results are usually positive. Negative words, negative results. More than half my students and clients have at some point in our conversations stated they were afraid of their homes – **afraid** of the dwelling which is to be the sacred, nurturing place for us to retreat to – that this home was the reason for all their misfortunes.

Why were they filled with fear of their home? Because they had heard from a friend or colleague, or read in a book that their home had "bad Feng Shui". I know this feeling, for when I heard that story from Professor Lin Yun, it made me feel terribly guilty and extremely disempowered, guilty that I had bought the house, guilty that I had arranged the rooms the way I did, and powerless to be able to change it. It filled me with doubt and fear, and I vowed I would **never** intentionally be the cause of that same doubt and fear in another human being!

The story takes drawings and explanations beyond the scope of this book. It haunted me for years, yet it taught me about the energies of our surroundings. For that I am eternally grateful. I want to share that gratitude with you so you, too, may benefit from its beauty. I want this book to be an inspiration for you, so please forgive me for not sharing this story since it could possibly create negative images for you, too, about this truly wonderful gift of knowledge regarding the creation of home.

I hope the questioning I went through to discover what this is all about, and its relevance on the design of our homes, will be of benefit to you. It brought me to a way of working with, and describing the theories that most people from a non-Buddhist, linear thinking society might be capable of understanding. There are parts of this philosophy that still don't make sense to me today, yet I have seen mild to miraculous changes, so I will share them with you so you can have this knowledge and make up your own mind.

Bringing this ancient knowledge into modern life

Feng Shui embraces principles of harmony and balance – a balance of a physical dwelling on the land and with its occupants. All are interconnected. If there is an imbalance in one, it is usually reflected in the other. In our culture, we do not often think of the interconnection.

Do you view a building as an extension of the land? Do you perceive yourself as an extension of your home?

Frank Lloyd Wright designed buildings that blended into the landscape, often repeating the rhythm of the space. One of his projects, the house at Falling Waters, is a perfect example. Using materials from the region to construct it, the colors blend with the palette of the landscape. Part of the house is built over a stream. The water falls over several large, flat boulders, and the descending balconies of concrete portray those boulders. The spirit of the land is repeated in the spirit of the home.

Feng Shui has been an oral tradition for thousands of years, between 4,000 and 17,000 years depending on what you read or who you listen to. It helps people become aware of their surroundings − their country, town, land, dwellings, furnishings and people − and the energies involved with each one along with the interaction of each to the other.

The words "Feng" and "Shui" refer to "wind" and "water" respectively, two types of energies and elements. These are the two elements that have shaped this land, forming the terrain of mountains, canyons, plains and caves. They are also the two elements we must have to live − air to breathe, water to drink.

We talk about energy in Feng Shui − the traditional word used is "chí." There are many types of energy − good, bad, negative, secret arrow, blocked and stuck, just to name a few. We all know that feeling of exuberance when we accomplish a goal or that "runner's high", when every part of you is working together in perfect harmony. That is good energy or ch'i. I will use the words chí and energy interchangeably. You have also had those really bad days when nothing seemed to go right and you felt drained after only a few hours. These too are examples of energy − examples of the vital force within you.

The land, dwellings and furnishings all have their own energy, plus they have combined energy. You can drive along a road, see an old farmhouse with a swing on the front porch and smile at the beauty and serenity. You can walk into a restaurant only to discover a dirty, dreary space and immediately walk out because it doesn't feel right. These are other examples of energy.

Feng Shui gathers this information of good and not-so-good energy of people, places, and things, and puts it together into guidelines to create harmonious environments for the occupants.

Ralph Waldo Emerson and Henry David Thoreau spoke of the harmony within nature, the spirit of each living thing and its relationship to the whole, and how all elements were in balance.

The ancient Chinese masters would look at the whole picture. They would find out when and where their client was born. They would look up the astrological and numerological aspects associated with the client to find the direction that would be the most beneficial for the person to sleep, locate the entrance to the dwelling, and placement of the doors.

These were not the only tools he would use. There would be other sciences consulted, although our society considers most of these the "occult" sciences. It was very involved and directed to the perfect location for one individual.

Then the masters would scour the countryside to find a mountain range that would protect their clients from the cold northern winds of winter, allow the tropical breezes to cool in summer, and provide for drinking and cleansing, as well as for soothing sounds and a beautiful view. This is called the "armchair position" because the mountain configuration is like sitting in a chair with a high mountain in back and lower mountains on the sides. One feels very protected, stable and balanced.

This position may also be called the dragon position since the mountain range often resembles the shape of a dragon. You know how revered the dragon is in China. Many festivals and ceremonies start with a dragon parade as the dragon is a symbol of good fortune.

Although many people would love to live in a place as described above, it is not possible for everyone, and some people prefer the more arid locations of the desert. No matter where we live, there is still the need for wind and water, as well as other elements, to sustain life.

Our modern buildings and high tech environments isolate us from the elements. They allow us to live and work in very hot or very cold areas, but often in buildings with few or no windows. The air we breathe is piped through tubes. We spend days, weeks or months without seeing much of the sun itself, particularly during the winter time of year. We become out of touch, out of balance with what is natural. However, by bringing certain objects into our structures, we can start to bring balance back into our lives.

The way we bring balance back into our structures is to look at the energies in and around them. By adding, subtracting or moving objects we can affect those energies. Sometimes we need to do something with colors, sometimes furniture or possibly something with one of the five elements.

Before we actually start to balance the energies with the Ba-Gua, let me share some insights into energies and some of the beliefs you may have heard about them. These examples may not be explained here exactly the way you have heard them described before, but they are being shared in a way that seems to get the gist of the information across to my students, clients and interior designers so they may use this knowledge most effectively.

You may have heard many Chinese will not buy a home on a T-intersection. The reasoning has to do with energy – too much energy bombarding the house. These homes seem to have a higher turnover than other homes in the same neighborhood.

Also sometimes Asian buyers want to know why a house is for sale. Is the family moving into a larger home because they have profited in this house or are they leaving because of misfortune? The homes on T-intersections seem to have a larger percentage of divorces, bankruptcies and illnesses than others in the neighborhood. Is this coincidence or "Bad Feng Shui"?

We do not have the answers at this time. Since this knowledge has been shared orally all these years, we don't have documentation. What if there is something to this "too much energy" concept? What if you could change the location of a door or re-landscape the front yard and by doing that could save families from the trauma of divorce, or bankruptcy or illness? Wouldn't it be worth the cost to research this further?

The way I like to explain the energy of a T-intersection house is like this: first of all, the placement of the home is at the center of the top of the T where you have one street that ends at another. The cars traveling along the street will stop before they enter the intersection if the brakes are correctly applied. If, however, they don't allow enough time – say they didn't allow for the oil rising from the street when it first starts to rain – the car may go through the intersection, onto the sidewalk, pass the landscaping and into the house. This very definitely is negative energy! We call it straight energy.

What are the chances of that happening, you might ask? I know several houses where it has happened anywhere from three to five times. Anyone who has had a house like that will tell you it only takes one time to be too much.

Let me share with you another kind of energy you get from automobiles. Light energy – the energy from the headlights shining into the windows of the homes on those T-intersection. This light energy becomes very irritating when you are working or reading in one of those rooms in front. Often people stop using these rooms, finding other areas of the house where they feel more protected. Then we say those rooms are "dead rooms" because they do not have the energy of human beings entering them.

Mini-blinds, verticals or shutters are often used in these rooms to make them feel safe, cutting out the headlight energy. At the same time, the people forget to open them in the morning for the first rays of sunlight. So they have accomplished the blockage of negative energy **and** at the same time blocked out the positive energy of the sun.

Feng Shui is the balance of "negative" and "positive", "yin" and "yang", "masculine" and "feminine". It is the *balance of the opposites.* This is a key point in using Feng Shui. We want balance. We are not stagnant. We are evolving. Transforming. Our homes need to reflect this change, evolution, transformation. What might be right for you today, may not be right for you next week, month or year because you are constantly changing.

Several of the other beliefs you might have heard regarding Feng Shui have to do with "straight energy". Having the front door in alignment with the back door. Having the stairs end where they are facing the front door. Having your bed with your feet in direct alignment to the bedroom door.

The belief here has to do with the concept of having a spirit, or vital energy force, within the body and the ability of that spirit to leave the body. The story goes like this. If you place the feet toward the door, the spirit will be pulled from the body. When you have doors in alignment, the spirit is pulled through the house too quickly. When walking down steps, the spirit is pulled off the last step and out the door even if the person wants to stay in the house.

These are rather far fetched beliefs for most Westerners to understand. but an interesting side note here. This belief originates from the Asian concepts of death and the ability of the spirit to leave the body at the time of death. They want the foot of the coffin to be in alignment with the door so the spirit might easily leave the room through the door and this plane or universe to transition to its next "assignment".

Our culture actually has a similar belief. Many of the funeral homes in the United States are set up with the foot of the coffin facing a door. Long ago I learned the saying "being carried out feet first" originated from this same belief.

Energy can be within a building, outside a building, in the landscape, or the vital force energy of the human occupants, just to name a few. The placement of all of these interplay on the other. Finding a balance is a lifetime endeavor.

Understanding the Ba-Gua

So where do we start?

Let's start with the Ba-Gua, what it looks like and how to work with it. It is an eight-sided object that originated from the I-Ching, or Book of Changes. In fact, the word "Ba" means "eight" and the word "Gua" means "sides", hence, "eight sides". It looks like an octagon when all the sides are even, but it can be stretched just like an octagon table might be stretched by adding leaves if you need to make it bigger.

Why do we want to know about the Ba-Gua? Because it tells us where the nine different areas of life are located within our dwellings. We need to know where the nine areas are located so we know if we have all nine areas in equal proportions to one another. If they are in proportion to each other, we will have balance on one level within the structure. If we do not, then we will know where we need to go to do the work to bring it into balance.

We use the Ba-Gua as though it is an overlay for a map, only it is used on floor plans of houses and rooms, lot plans, maps of apartment-type complexes, and smaller areas such as desks. Depending upon the geographical origin of the philosophy, the next step varies. I have found the easiest one for most people to grasp, that brings positive results, suggests you locate the Ba-gua according to the orientation of the door (Figure 1).

I personally like this idea of the door being the focal point of orientation since it transitions you from one location to another – the threshold – whether it is from the outdoors in, or from one room to another. Another reason for my preference for the door-orientation is the significance doors and doorways play in our lives. They are a barrier from things not wanted and a welcome to "the good things in life". They are symbolic of communication – the ability to speak, be heard, and understood.

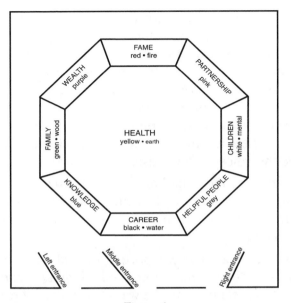

Figure 1.

In using the door-orientation method, you want to stand in the doorway, looking into the room. This wall where the doorway is located becomes the "entrance" wall that is the wall containing the three areas of knowledge, career, and helpful people. Using the main entrance door, you will always enter the room or building in one of these three areas. You may have other doors in the room, but what you are wanting is a flow of energy from the street to your **front** door, then travel the most direct route to the door of each room within the structure. We want the most "chí" possible to come to each of the rooms without obstruction.

The reason we use the front door verses the garage, side or back door is due, again, to the significance of doors. Doors signify the voice of the adult. This is the area where you greet people who visit. This is where they first get to see who you are, what you are like, how you perceive the world. Front doors equal the first words out of you mouth. Is it clean, fresh smelling, bright and shiny like freshly brushed teeth?

Did you know there are many home buyers of Asian descent who will count the number of working doors (including sliding doors, closet doors, bedroom doors ... all doors) and then count the number of moving windows (sliding, crank, opening skylights ... moveable windows) to find out which number is larger? The reason behind this one lies in the belief that doors are the voice of the adult and windows are the voice of the child. If there are more windows than doors, the children will have the voice in the house.

This may sound stupid or ridiculous to you, but the next time you enter a household of unruly children ... count the doors and windows. You, too, will be surprised at the coincidence in this belief.

Front doors are more important than all the other doors. We had front doors long before we had garages and interior rooms with doors on them. We want to direct all the energy to the front door so people can find us – so the positive ch'i can find us.

Using the doorway as the entrance into the Ba-Gua shows you the voice of the room. If you enter a room through the knowledge area door, you are picking up energy of learning or teaching. Whenever I teach classes, if I have a choice among rooms, I prefer rooms with doors in either the knowledge or helpful people areas rather than the career area. When we all enter through career, in general, the classes seem to be more focused on careers. With helpful people they seem to be more into helping mankind, and the doorway of knowledge classes seem to be more learning oriented.

The next step in figuring out the placement of the areas of life requires you to imagine a division of the room into thirds in both directions – divide it lengthwise and widthwise into thirds (Figure 2). If your room is either a perfect square or rectangle in shape – no closets, bathrooms or kitchens sticking into it or cut out of it – then you will have nine smaller versions of the larger room. They will be either squares or rectangles. If your room is irregular in shape, you will need to use some of the guidelines listed a couple of paragraphs later.

Let's draw a visual for you. Starting at 12 o'clock and moving clockwise are the areas of (1) fame, (2) partnership and marriage, (3) children, (4) helpful people/benefactors, (5) career, (6) knowledge, (7) family, and (8) wealth. The center is the ninth area, encompassing all other aspects of life and health. The Ba-gua can be applied to one room, to your apartment or house, your lot, your city, your continent. Feng Shui

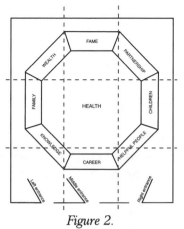

Figure 2.

affects every aspect of the environment – even your workplace and your vehicle.

Let's pretend we are walking in the front door of your home or apartment. In the middle of the farthest outside wall that is straight ahead, picture 12 o'clock, the area of fame. Mentally overlay the octagon onto your floor plan. In what area does your door appear? What room does wealth lie within? Where is partnership?

Since everyone learns in different ways, let's take another look at the room. Say the door is in the center of the room. You walk up to the door, open it and step onto the threshold. You are entering the room in the career area. The area to your right is the area of helpful people, the 4:30 position on a clock face. To your left is knowledge with a 7:30 position.

Continuing around the room clockwise we have the 9:00 position the area of family. At the 10:30 position we have wealth – it is always in the far left corner of the room. The fame area is located at 12 o'clock. In the 1:30 position we have partnership – it is always in the far right corner of a room as you enter the room – with the children's area located in the 3 o'clock position. We are back to the 4:30 position of helpful people. The center of the clock – the pivotal point of the hands – is the area of health.

Again we use this Ba-Gua as on overlay on the whole house, again in each room, and it can even be used on your desk. We always look for the door – what we call the "mouth of chi" – to help us orient and position the Ba-gua.

When the room or house is square or rectangular, it is relatively easy. When the house is irregular in shape we need to find out if we have all parts or what we might have extra or be missing. Again, there are several ways to approach this and my students say the following way has helped them to work with the Ba-gua most easily.

Wherever the door is located, that will become the "front wall" of the house for placement of the Ba-Gua. Pretend you are standing in that doorway right now, about to enter the house. The subconscious mind is saying that wall is the front of the house. It draws an imaginary line running from the doorway along the wall to the point of the house that extends the most to the left and right of the house.

Next we need to locate the side walls. They will be the farthest walls to the left and right of the house when you are looking at the house floor plan – the outside walls. This wall may, or may not, be connected to the front wall. The house might "jog" forward or backward before it reaches that "farthest distance" outside wall (Figures 3 and 4).

If the jog creates an extra space in front of the house, like many attached garages do, then you will have "extra" in an area (Figure 3). If the jog moves toward the back of the house, you will have a hole or "missing" piece (Figure 4).

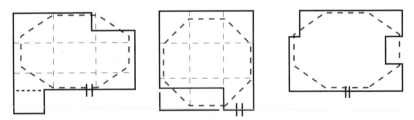

Figure 3, Figure 4, and Figure 5.

Since many homes have been remodeled, you may have several "jogs" in this wall, or line, that runs from the front to the back of the house. If you do, you will usually be "missing" a little bit of some areas. Please do not worry at this time about any missing areas. We will be able to remedy the "missing pieces" when you start to accessorize you home. The accessories become the missing pieces that personalize the remedy. They are very important and powerful.

Once you have figured out the placement of the side walls, we can find the back of the house. If there is one straight wall, it is easy to locate the back, but any "jogs" here challenge us to measure the lengths of each. We are looking for the longest wall and preferably its length will be more than half the total width. Henceforth, if you have three or more different "back" walls, you will want to measure each one. Then you will total all of those that are in alignment with another. This will be the "back-of-the-house" wall (Figures 6 and 7).

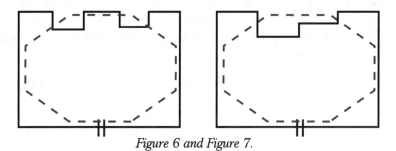

Figure 6 and Figure 7.

This "back-of-the-house" wall becomes very important as it helps us define the back side of the Ba-Gua. This allows us to place the Ba-Gua on the house plan so we can figure out if we have "extra" or "missing" pieces in the back of our house. If there is a vacant space between the "front" wall and the "back" wall, you are "missing" a piece. If there is something sticking out beyond this back wall, you have "extra" energy in that area. If you have a part of the house sticking out in front of the front wall, then you will have extra energy – energy that is considered to be "outside-the-house" (Figure 3).

To determine if you are missing parts of an area on the side, we need to look at the side lines. If the side lines are straight on the floor plan – going from the front wall of the house to the back wall without jogging – then you have complete areas. If the line has a jog in it, then you will be missing part of an area, since you will have used the wall that extends out the furthest from the side of the house as the side of the Ba-Gua (Figure 5). You will not have any "extra" areas on the side unless you have a bow or bay window. They create small "extra" pieces (Figure 8).

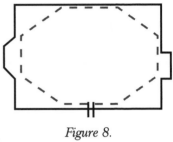

Figure 8.

Now that we have learned how to place the Ba-Gua on a house floor plan, determining where the front and back lines of the house are located, the sides and if we have extra or missing areas – we can locate the nine areas of energy within the house and rooms that are located in those areas. The reason for locating these areas is to determine if your physical house is balanced.

Balancing your home using the Ba-Gua

Balancing the physical house will allow you to balance the other aspects of your life – the mental, emotional and spiritual. Remember the four levels of health as stated in the chapter that describes the areas of the Ba-Gua. It says the health area relates to physical, mental, emotional and spiritual. If the physical house is out-of-balance, then you will be working harder at life trying to get the physical into balance. This drains you of energy. Let me give you a couple of examples.

If your house is physically missing a part of the wealth area, your mental mind realizes it. It becomes focused on issues around money. The mind becomes fixated on the "missing" piece of your physical house and says "missing money", or a lack of money. No matter what you do, it keeps saying, "lack, lack, lack" because the house is lacking that energy.

We want to change that thought pattern, so we "fill in" the area. We can fill in the missing part by building an addition onto the house. "What do you do if you are renting the home or live in a condo or apartment?" you might ask. You cannot build on the missing part, but you can bring in the missing energy in several ways.

First, we could hang a mirror on the inside of the room on the wall adjoining the missing area. This is one of the common "cures". We could plant a tree outside where the two walls would have intersected to complete that missing part of the house creating the wealth area. Or we could find the wealth area of the room closest to the wealth area of the house, or the wealth area of any other room within the house, and bring something symbolic of "your wealth" into that area.

You are now performing a simple ceremony, or ritual, to change the energy of "missing wealth" in order to bring new energy into that space – attracting wealth to your home. This is done through the power of intention. The "Power of Intention", or the "Power of Your Mind," will change the energy your mind is creating. Your "Intention" focuses your "Attention" on the desired outcome. By placing an object that symbolizes wealth in an area of wealth, you are filling the void with an object (physical) so your mind will now see this area filled – focusing attention on a completed and balanced physical dwelling.

Then the Universe gets to do its part. Do you remember the statement "The Universe abhors a vacuum"? Now the Universe thinks you have a hole that needs to be filled because you started to fill it – physically. Before there was a lack mentality – you were "missing" it. You have focused your mind, your positive attention, "to fill the void", so the Universe will do its part "to fill the void". This will work for all areas of your home and life.

Another example I love to share is my own house. My homes have been my greatest teachers because I have to live with them and solve the challenges as they arise in my life.

When I moved into my current house, as I have shared, I had a lot of clutter. I had been working to clear it for several months. Life was not much fun. I was dealing with the legal issues of the divorce, working a part-time job, starting another new business of my own in design (I was legally ending a previous business partnership), and was going to school. I really wanted a special person I could share my life with as well as end the legal issues of the divorce and design partnership.

I knew my house was out-of-balance. I had not taken the time to really measure the back wall to see if I had extra wealth energy or if I was missing partnership. Sure enough, when I measured the two back walls, they were close in length. The back left wall was about 6" longer than the right. That meant the left half of the house would be used as the back wall. I was missing all of Partnership, part of Fame, part of Children and part of Health.

I had little money, so remodeling was out of the question. I went outside to see what I might possibly do. Finding a peach tree close to the intersecting point, I decided to use it as a large stabilizing force. When there is this much of an area "missing," we need to create stability to the area. Then I found a stone in the yard and moved it to the exact intersection. I knew this completion of the area would work. I also knew there were many different possibilities in the outcomes that could occur. I needed to focus my intention on the outcomes I wanted.

The next thing I did was go inside the house. I created an altar in the partnership area of my bedroom. It was just a small bookcase with a drop-leaf desk, but it became a focal point of the qualities I wanted in my life. It contained:

1) *A list of 200 qualities I wanted in the man of my dreams*

2) *A list of 200 qualities I had to give in the relationship*

3) *A candle to signify my light and the energy of fire*

4) *Two pink flowers in a beautiful vase*

5) *A picture of my parents on their 25th Anniversary*

6) *A book on the power of prayer and healing*

7) *An angel*

8) *A picture of my children (located on the back cover)*

9) *An empty picture frame*

Symbology has great power on the subconscious mind. In this process I was using a great deal of symbology. Both lists of qualities showed I had given great thought to what I wanted in my life and what I had to offer in the relationship. The candle was a aromatherapy candle with a fragrance that has powerful meaning to me. The flowers, being pink, represented partnership. The picture of my parents' 25th anniversary was meant to represent a long term relationship. The empty frame was to allow space for a picture of my soon-to-be loved one and me.

I lit the candle, played some romantic music, sang, and dreamed that evening. The next day, it was back to the regular activities of life, letting go of any preconceived ideas regarding the outcomes.

Three days later, Hilory – now my loved one and soul mate – came into my life. Of course I didn't know he was my soul mate at the time, but after eight wonderful years together, I can say he is the one. The one whose qualities were listed in my journal. The one who makes my light shine by bringing out the best in me.

A week later the last few legal issues were resolved in the partnerships and I began to have more time and fun in my life. When I did this whole process, I was still in a state of doubt regarding some aspects of the beliefs involved in ceremonies and the different Ba-Gua energies. This personal experience was one of many that have convinced me of the enormous power of our dwellings and the incredible power behind ceremonies.

If you are new to it like I was, questioning it, I am glad, because I feel you need to have your own experience of it. Be willing to try it. Massage it. Play with it. Do a little at a time. If things go the way you want, great! Continue! If it doesn't, then stop and try something else.

Everyone is different and we need to honor those differences. If we don't, it can create difficulties.

For instance, one lady had read in a book on Feng Shui that she should hang hollow reeds (bamboo flutes) from the beams to prevent those beams from weighing down on her while she was in bed. She went to Chinatown to find them and hung them in her bedroom. Her husband disliked them so much, an argument ensued. More and more tension arose because of the flutes.

In a desperate state, she called me. I suggested she twine an artificial ivy along the beam or make a canopy above the head of her bed. Both of those worked for both her and her husband.

Another person had placed her bed in the direction best suited for her. It made her husband feel very uncomfortable. They started to argue. I suggested they compromise and place the bed in the "armchair" position.

The armchair position is the location within a room that is furthest from the door. The easiest way I have found to describe this is to think back to the times we lived in caves. We would place ourselves as far from the opening of the cave as possible while still being able to see the entrance. This way we could watch the opening, feeling comfortable with the view so we could grab a spear or gun to protect ourselves from a predator should one enter. Taking this concept into a bedroom, the position would be to have the bed as far from the door as possible yet be able to see the door. This worked for them.

When we are in relationship with one or more people, we need to consider them as well as ourselves. In most marriages or "significant other" partnerships, we have attracted our opposite into our lives to help balance us. If we place the bed in **my** ideal location, chances are it will be one of **their** least ideal positions. The saying "Do unto others as you would have them do unto you" really applies here.

Energy, the Ba-Gua and Floor Plans

Let's take the concept of the armchair position into the living room and family rooms. When we are sitting in a room relaxing, reading or watching TV, we will feel most at ease when we can see someone coming toward us. We don't want the traffic pattern in the room to come up behind us because we can become easily startled. Ideally this would mean we would arrange the seating to look at the entrance.

Often, we have a focal point in the room and we are taught in design school to arrange the seating areas to face this focal point. Using the armchair position to look at the entrance might be in direct conflict with the desire to use the focal point of the room. Again, we need to make choices.

Some of the questions we need to ask are:

What is the use of the room?

How often does it get used?

Is there only one person who uses it or one person at a time?

Will there be many people using it?

Is it the main area for the family to come together?

Each room and occupant situation is different. If you are alone in the space with your back to the door looking at a magnificent view, you could be daydreaming when someone comes up behind you, scaring you tremendously. This would not be good. Can you arrange the chair, sofa or chaise so you might be able to see both the entrance and the view out of your peripheral vision? Could you put a screen or sofa table behind you that will make the person come around in front of you?

If it is a room with lots of people and activities going on, you may want to make a conscious decision to place the most alert person in the family where they can see someone entering. You might place a mirror or some kind of reflective surface so you can see if someone is approaching. The more focused or fixated you are on the task at hand, the more easily you will be startled.

Children are generally less likely to be startled than older adults. Maybe it is because they are using their sixth sense. Who knows? Sometimes elderly people who are hard of hearing become frightened easily. We want to increase people's enjoyment of life and feel safe and nurtured.

An office situation is the same. We want to be as far from the door as possible while being able to view the door. Facing the view can mean you have your back to the door. Very often desks in the cubical offices are placed with not only the back to the door, but facing a wall. Here, the person is not only easily startled, but they become blocked as well.

Whenever we have a wall within 6 feet of the human body, the subconscious mind decides we are being blocked. Sitting at a desk with a wall 30" from us can make us feel stymied in some area of our life. What can we do? We can put a mirror on the wall in front of us to help us see what is coming toward us. We might also want to put a landscape picture with depth – a meadow, mountain range, ocean – giving you the sense of more depth of possibilities.

As a call to awareness of your space, if your desk is piled with papers, the mirror might make you feel you have twice the work load if you can see the piles in the mirror. You might be better served to place a beautiful landscape picture above your desk, especially if it has meaning to you, like a vacation dreamland.

Anytime you are walking and are faced with a wall within 6 feet of your body, you are experiencing a feeling of blocked energy. As you become more aware of it, you will recognize how many of these we encounter each day at work, home, and shopping. The only ones we have any control over are the ones at home, so we want to improve these places as much as possible.

Mirrors can be placed on any of these walls with a word of caution. Always look at *all* the things that are to be reflected in those mirrors. If you see trash, clutter, sharp objects, stairs or another wall, you probably would be better served to place a magnificent landscape there instead.

Landscapes connect us to the nature. They can gently guide us when we come to a wall. If the only direction we can travel when we reach the wall is to the right, it can lead us down a road that goes to the right. A wall where we can only turn left, will need a picture with a stream or road that meanders to the left. If you can go both directions, we need something that will guide us both directions, like animals walking both directions or cars moving in both directions.

Landscapes bring into the concrete, structured, manmade world of the building the essence of a Higher Power. This is the blending of the masculine with the feminine, the linear/logical with the non-linear/intuitive, the yang with the yin. This is what we are working towards, the balance of the opposites. It is this balancing that makes our homes comfortable, nurturing and sacred.

We want to make our homes a nurturing, comfortable place for all who enter in love, and a sacred place for our own spirit and soul. Exploring the Ba-Gua with its intricacies as they relate to your home will take time, energy and patience. It is this time, energy and patience that will be given back to you in myriad ways creating the sacred balance you desire in your life.

"For as you give, so shall you reap."

"*Walk through the different rooms where you eat, sleep, and live, Bless the walls, the roof, the windows and the foundation. Give thanks for your home exactly as it exists today; sift and sort, simplify, and bring order to the home you have. Realize that the home of your dream dwells within.*"

Sarah Ban Breathnach

Closets, Collections, and Clutter

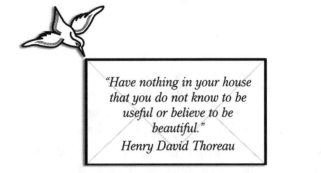

Several months ago I cleaned my bedroom. It was a very thorough job including the dresser drawers and closets. It took me several days and I vowed at that time I would stay on top of it. I know the impact of clutter on the mind, how the filled closet is symbolic of a filled life, hence, no more room for good opportunities to come one's way. Before I started, the closet door wouldn't even close, and since doors are symbolic of communications, that might mean I would have to work harder with my communication in order to heard or understood.

"Real Life" often happens to me, and I bet it happens to you. Why don't we take the time to keep our bedrooms looking and feeling like the sanctuaries they are meant to be? It always makes us feel so good, we have so much more energy, and it soothes our soul. Sometimes it is because we are ill, or too tired, or we just decide the one or two things we aren't going to put away won't impact us for the day or two they left out. Usually, it's because we are in a hurry.

Items we own can also become "heavy anchors" in our lives. We live in a society driven by material accumulations. Advertisements through various medias tell us we will feel better, have more fun, gain great success, and have that incredibly romantic relationship, if only we buy this product or that service. I don't know about you, but these have never been a "quick fix" solution for me. How very sad for our society to have traveled so far from the real riches of life –

having quality time with our loved ones, quality time for ourselves to reflect on the many blessings we have, and quality time to develop a closer connection with the heart and soul of who we are, our spirituality.

There is no doubt we need certain items for our daily lives, and it is nice to "allow ourselves" special "treats" once in a while, but if it becomes an obsession, and we are out of control, or if it makes us do things we later regret, then it might be time to seek the help of professionals.

Experience has shown me the "negative" energy tied to some of what we have. We often fight to get a certain object in a divorce. We buy something we cannot afford to impress someone else or build our self-esteem, then we go to *one more seminar or class* that will teach us how to straighten up our lives, not truly believing and knowing we might already have the answer within. All of these eat away at our God-given qualities.

I will never forget the statement I heard by a woman as she watched her home burn after the 1989 Loma Prieta Earthquake in northern California. Although the only possessions she was able to save were the clothes she wore, she said, "I feel so free. Nothing can hold me back anymore. I can go where I want, anytime I want."

I thought she was crazy on one level, and I envied her on another. For you see, I had also experienced that same earthquake, but was feeling so glad my house had survived. I was definitely tied to the value of the house and the items in it – filled with fear of survival – that I was fighting for them in a divorce, compromising many of my beliefs. I was not far enough on my spiritual path to trust I would be loved and cared for by the Great Creator I had been raised to believe in.

I had so many things I didn't have room for them all. I wanted things I had no use for. Actually, there were things I wanted that didn't fit who I was any longer, but I wanted them just the same.

Has anything like that ever happened to you? Have you recently gone through your closet to see what clothes still fit or are in style? Do you have material to sew, yet haven't sat at a machine for 5 years (can you even locate where it is)? Or, how about that collection of frames sitting on a table with pictures of your friends that hasn't been dusted in weeks?

Do you have any idea how these are making you feel on a subconscious level? Several of these are aspects we deal with in Feng Shui.

Closets are a place to put things we need and use occasionally, like clothes and linens. We do not wear the same outfit each day, so in-between wearings they hang there. The table linens and towels for different occasions are available for us to see and reach when they are needed. Sometimes these closets hold boxes filled with tax papers or Christmas decorations. When they get to the point of overflowing, they are draining you of energy.

Closets need to be organized space, not an accident waiting to happen. When we have so much we can't find what we need when we need it, we probably have too much. But how do we decide what to keep, what to throw away, where to store it and how to find it?

At this point I would like to share an article I wrote in the early 90's that was published in an international publication. It tells a story of my journey including personal tragedies, lost hopes, feelings, help and hope. I have left it unedited from that time so you might see the growth in personal style and self-esteem. These are important qualities for each of us to acknowledge and support in our brothers and sisters.

Organize Your Life by Linda Lenore, published in The Reporter, September 1993

This wasn't a maze. It was a tunnel to a tomb with no way out. Boxes were everywhere: entry, attic, eating nook, bedrooms and living, family, laundry rooms. Even the playhouse, garage, two patios and part of the yard, were filled with boxes. No place else to put them and I already had one storage unit! This much stuff, and it was only half, "my half". These boxes of emotional dynamite were everywhere you turned. Sometimes the explosion of emotional turmoil would erupt.

As depressing, overwhelming, and sad as the first part of this story is, I share it with you to help you experience, and possibly understand, my frame of mind. I know I am not alone in these experiences, for others have shared with me. My hope is to help others who find themselves in any of these situations. Also to let you know of the birth of a new career field, Professional Organizers, to help people work through all sorts of clutter or improve their current paper and work flow. Our society makes us deal with the logical part of death and dying. In order to do so, most of us have to shut out the emotional aspects so we can cope.

It seemed hopeless to ever get through all of these boxes, remainders of the pain, sorrow, and lost dreams. I had fought hard to get this much in the divorce, not even close to half, but at least I had the things that mattered most to me – my mother's furniture and prized possessions, things of Jeff, my son, had made or owned, and gifts given to me. I deserved all of this and more. I would work hard for them. Not only was I bitter and angry, I was tired. I felt unimportant. I wanted to have a career, a great job, a home, a man in my life. I couldn't stand to be at home. It wasn't home: I had moved. No friends here, they all lived 40 miles away. I had made the choice to give up that life-style. Now that it had happened, it wasn't what I had pictured. I was depressed and confused about myself, my ability to do anything, especially my ability to do paperwork, to organize, to clean my house, much less be able to decorate it. And my business was interior design. Not only was it depressing to have my space look like this, it was demoralizing. I did not love to make other people's space beautiful any longer. I resented them for having time, money, energy and help to achieve this. After all these years of working in this field (my only true source of income). I did not "feel" like helping others.

That was at the tail end of the spiral downward. It started in 1984 when my mother was diagnosed with Jacob-

Creuztfeldt Disease. We were good friends. She had moved close to us to see her grandchildren on a regular basis. She had been alert, lively, and a positive thinker. Now she was confused, accusatory and ill. I had no tools to deal with this. My father had died when I was 15. I learned very quickly that our society believes in hiding grief and sorrow. We are expected to be back to school or work in 3 days, maybe a week if you are not a strong person.

Mom's health was so bad and my family life so dysfunctional, my only thought was a nursing home for her where she would be cared for, but only if I went there everyday. Scandals were emerging on the neglect that abounded in nursing homes. I stayed for hours to bath, clothe and feed her. I felt myself an incompetent, terrible daughter who should be caring for her at my home.

Meanwhile, my husband had started yet another remodeling project on our home. Every room was dismantled. Plaster dust was everywhere. Anything we valued was covered or put out of sight. Finally, Mom died. It was a relief in many ways, but the guilt remained. No time to grieve. I was now the executor for her estate, a new experience for me, which meant dealing with the magnitude of red tape for medical bills. The endless hours of sorting and disposing of her three bedroom house filled with furniture, memorabilia, and junk. Luckily the delightful English couple next door had purchased a home and wanted to buy mom's furniture. What angels they were! Mom loved them from the moment they moved here from England. Plus, my son Jeff, and their son James, were now best friends. So I could still see and enjoy Mom's furniture. Then her home was cleaned out and rented.

Paper work now demanded immediate attention. We finished up a few projects so I had a room to devote to it. Then the fire in the Los Gatos hill occurred. One friend asked to bring her possessions and cats to stay with us. She used that room. When the fire was finally put out, my friend's house being spared, kitten and caboodle were moved back to their home.

For the next month things moved slowly. My husband was starting up his business. Jeff was feeling his independence at age 13, riding the trains with his grandfather. Melanie, my daughter, was exploring her freedom having just received her "learner's permit" to drive. My life was manageable.

Then Labor day weekend arrived. Jeff had a severe headache all weekend long. We were in and out of the emergency room everyday. A very alert nurse who was there persuaded the doctor to do a CAT scan. It revealed a blood clot. The same neurologist who had diagnosed my mother's disease performed the surgery. Jeff came through with flying colors.

Of course, I spent everyday with him. He came home and I started back on the paperwork. Now it included the medical bills for Jeff. Although Jeff had appeared to be fine, subsequent CAT scans showed differently. In early November, Jeff had a second surgery. I'll never forget the doctor's face or voice when he said Jeff had a malignant tumor and might only live 2 months. Jeff died 2 days later. The rage and emotions I felt . . . terror, anger, disbelief, sadness, desperation. How, why was this happening?

The holidays were now upon us, but there was no way any of us felt like participating. The letter we sent to people shared the traumas of our life. It did not reflect the true picture at all. Many times I contemplated suicide. Any belief in God had been shattered. The only thing that kept me going was the love I had for Melanie. My husband, Burt, was hiding his grief in his new company. I truly had no selfworth.

At this time I also needed to write thank you notes for memorial gifts, sort and do paperwork for medical bills and taxes. The medical community, state and federal governments, and most people did not understand the emotional state I was in. I played ostrich for a long time. Only when I was made to come out of my hole and do it by a regulated time frame or verbal abuse did I work on it.

Finally, friends of mine started to help me. First, there was the building up of my self-esteem by an employer. Second, a friend helped me to sort some of Mom's possessions. Next, a plea for "Toys for Tots" from a fire station that had been robbed at Christmas allowed Melanie and me to pack the van to overflowing with Jeff's old toys.

All this helped, but another issue was fast becoming obvious. The marriage was more than rocky, it was over. I filed for divorce.

The next year was even harder. Now I was faced with not only maintaining the house, but fixing it up to sell. It was even harder to do day-to-day paperwork. I put it off. I didn't go through the mail. I couldn't pay the bills, so why should I open them up? I was in total denial as to the magnitude of the problem. I painted till 2 or 3 in the morning, went to bed, and got up at 5:30 AM to go to work. I rented two storage units to put all the extra things so the house would look uncluttered. (The 4-car garage, including the rafters, was filled to the top with stuff, not cars).

We put the house, in a little community next to Los Gatos, California, on the market to sell in October. The house was painted and as of 4:30 PM on October 17, the house was clean (the cleaning crew having just left). We were ready for the Realtor's open house the next morning. At 5:04 PM the earthquake hit. Things tumbled from closets and cupboards. The furniture fell over, water sloshed out of the pool, we lost power, but we were all alive. I finally arrived home some 90 minutes and 10 miles later to find Melanie and my roommate cleaning up the mess. I was a basket case. My whole life was reflected in that earthquake's shaking, cracking, and caving in.

The next two months were frenetic. The house sold (it was solidly built and clean), and we packed, without sorting, into boxes, some labeled, some not. The movers came and moved all my things from that house to this new house.

Months after moving, here I was living in this dwelling filled with emotional dynamite, when my friend Pam says she would like to trade my design skills for her organizational skills. I had felt sorting the boxes and my emotions was my job and mine alone to do. This way I could play the martyr and also use excuses for not tending to it. I also did not know how to ask for help, much less accept it. But Pam and I have shared much of life's joys and sorrows. So very reluctantly we started. She planned a full day. It took just an hour to decide where to start. We surveyed all of it. We started in the master bedroom so that when I went to sleep my subconscious knew I was in a clean space. We got apple boxes with tops and bottoms. The categories were: a box for things to keep, one for "to go to another room", still another for give away, and an "I can't get rid of that yet" box, a box of "I can't deal with this today" and a box for throwaways. As a box became full, she labeled it. All "A" boxes, i.e. A-1, A-2, A-3, were Christmas decorations. She made up cards listing what was in each box so I could go to the file box and look for something rather than open each box which might have some unstable emotional dynamite. We went through about 8 of the 175 or so boxes.

I found when I was sorting through things with a friend, I could work faster. I didn't get stuck on what to do. She would ask me certain questions that would help to either put things in perspective or allow me to release emotions. Allowing the tears to flow or sharing a happy remembrance was strange and terrifying. So many people would say "Be strong," or "It's been so long, why are you still feeling that way?" Few people realize the grief process or know how to allow another human being to express feelings. The boxes were the cork holding my spirit inside from truly shining through. Each experience that was hurtful had pushed that cork farther and farther down. I was creating more and more stress and my body was now showing signs of it. My yearly physical revealed medical problems.

When Pam first started to help me, neither one of us really understood the importance to my life of what she was helping me do. As we worked throughout the day, I would cry and laugh. The old negative memories were being replaced with fun ones. The room was starting to be cleared. I felt good about it. When she finally had to leave, she asked if I was O.K.? I told her yes, which I basically thought I was. Looking back, I was exhausted. All the physical work was minor compared to the emotional work.

I continued to sort and clean well into the night. The next few days I wanted to sleep. But there were things to do. So I got up and did them. As time progressed and my knowledge increased as to what my body was saying, I learned to spend a few days after each major effort just pampering me. I would read, go to the beach, walk, or listen to music.

I started to share my experiences with people. While many have gone through similar experiences, few have been allowed to share them. I was able to speak to groups, to be real about who I was and what had happened. I found an acceptance for my speaking ability.

One coach encouraged me to share and another suggested I get involved in hospice. I did both. I volunteered and learned to be a grief counselor at The Center For Living With Dying in the San Jose area. As I shared my knowledge with Pam, we realized that as we worked together, she was allowing me to grieve while accomplishing the organizing and releasing of the old.

I remember a visit I had made to The Center shortly after Jeff's death. Maryann said, "Do not ignore the pictures your mind sees regarding the deaths in your life. Acknowledge them, hold them until they are ready to leave and replace them with a beautiful part of the life with the same people or places.

I now realize how valuable that advice had been. I could acknowledge the death bed scenes. Then, not dwelling on them, remember a time of love and joy. All this was allowing me to acknowledge my pain, working through it and grow into the new life I was making.

My new life has lead me to help others this same way and find others who also do this. Instead of selling products to people who many times were buying things as a substitute for lack of intimacy and love in their lives, I now help people to better utilize the things they have, often finding new home for them. Sometimes that means throwing it away. Most of the time though, we give it to useful causes. Sometimes it is loved by someone in the family, and now they can enjoy it. Once in while we find a place in the same home to give it less or more importance.

I'm still learning how to do this, and I'm still sorting through my own house with the boxes. It's the third or fourth pass and it's down to around 30 boxes, all of which are stored very nicely into the two car garage.

Light is at the end of the tunnel. I found professional organizers to be the guiding lights along the way. Just as I seem to stumble, one is there guiding me on a short cut, or sometimes leading me through a beautiful scenic route I would not have normally taken. They have helped me with clutter, office organization, space planning, financial organization, taxes, medical records, insurance, and death and dying issues, like finding wills, executorships and power of attorney. (This lady calls her business Exit Stage Right. You leave this stage the right way with things in order). There may be a need in your life to seek help of this nature. You may also have a gift to help others in this fashion, not realizing there is a need, much less a profession out there.

I have shared with you a journey from a dark, defeating dwelling to a sunlit, lighthearted, healing home filled with love, peace and joy. (I am now referred to as *The Healing Decorator*, and my home reflects this). As I shared earlier, I hope your life's journey never exposes you to these heartaches and traumas. Yet if it does, please know that I encourage you to seek the help of friends, or possibly a professional. It certainly has changed my life.

The gifts I have received are many. The peace and serenity of my own place is most precious. Closely following is the joy I receive when another person's self esteem is raised as they start to tackle this overwhelming, depressing situation we as a culture have created and ignore. Lastly, the many friends I have found are empowering, both those in the field of organizing and those I have helped organize.

God does work in mysterious ways. I love it!

* * * * * * * *

The above article still stirs emotions in me after all these years. I realize many of the "problems" I had in my life at that time were the results of my own actions and thinking process. I had never really understood the power of the mind. When I was happy, the world was happy. When I was sad, the world was sad. But I never understood it was my attitude that created my reality.

My "fighting" for items created all sorts of negative energy around me. I had many negative thinking friends in my life. We attracted each other and we fed off each others dramas in life.

The therapist I finally found to help me was a wonderful woman who nurtured my body, mind and spirit. She was a true professional as well as a very special wise person. She listened and guided me, making suggestions for me to explore. Slowly I found more and more "positive" thinking people to be with.

One of the things I have observed about positive thinkers, they don't stay stuck in the muck! They get on with life. Clutter is a sign we are "stuck". It slows us down, blocks our path, keeps us tied to the past. If we are going to be tied to the past, I want mine to be tied to the good memories I have shared with friends and family. For that I don't need items. Not even the most precious of family photos, for they can weigh you down if they were taken at a bad or sad time. No, I would not like to lose the pictures of my friends and family in a fire, but I have found that the good memories of loved ones whom I'm no longer with – my mother, father, son and ex-husband – can never be taken away from me. You know that too. We just forget once in awhile what our real needs are.

Do you collect things? My grandmother collected everything – jars, rubber bands, newspapers, fabric, magazines. She had an excuse. She lived during the depression when everything was difficult to come by and costly when you found it, so she saved everything. We would visit her at least once a week and the clutter never bothered me.

Now I shutter at the thought of her place because I see myself in her. The house was filled with boxes, but she could always find what she needed. I guess she was organized and I hope that trait is hereditary.

She also had collections everywhere. There were dolls and glass figurines, vases and porcelain ladies, quilts and crocheted dollies. No space was spared – not a shelf, cupboard, table or floor. Collections or clutter?

What constitutes a collection? Do you have one, two, twenty-two? How do you display them? What is the meaning or reason for the collection? Do you really enjoy your collection? Does your family or do your friends contribute to them?

Collections can fall into the same category as clutter without us realizing it. A collection is three or more of something and there usually is a reason for collecting it. You love the artist, styling, symbology, memories, or just the thrill of finding and adding it to the collection. Clutter is when the collection takes up your life and your space and dominates you, instead of you it. Have you conveyed to your loved ones why you have these collections and the role they play in your life?

Communicating the significance your collection plays in your life is imperative. When my mother died, my friend Jan came over to help me go through her furnishings. While boxing and sorting, she discovered there were pieces of what is called "depression glass". I had never heard about depression glass until Jan told me she had become interested in it a few years earlier. She loved the colorful glass salt and pepper shakers.

I did not really like nor appreciate antiques back then, so when she started to frequent the shows I listened as she described her "finds." They didn't excite me, but she was thrilled, so I was mildly happy for her. Now here she was telling me I had just inherited some of this "stuff". Great!!! How valuable was it? What was the reason it was called "depression glass"? Should I keep it or get rid of it?

Jan explained the story behind it. Sometimes they were "giveaways" in the box of laundry detergent, other times you got them as giveaways at the movies. Most were easy to find and rather inexpensive, not being true antiques (until now). But I found one of Mom's patterns was a little on the rare side and since I loved the color, I decided to go with Jan to the next show.

For several years we traveled almost every week to a different place throughout Northern California looking and buying. I got "hooked" on collecting. I bought depression glass and candlesticks. My daughter, Melanie, started to travel with us and became interested in Disney memorabilia. This was great. We developed an even deeper relationship through the many hours we spent together, all three of us.

I do not have all the "collections" now. I don't need them. They served their purpose — time together to talk and share. I still have the original pieces and a few candlesticks — I love to spend my nights by candlelight! Melanie still has some of her Disney cookie jars — she loves to bake. And Jan, well, she still has her salt and pepper shakers — they're displayed in a garden window where the sunlight shines on them creating the affect of a beautiful stained-glass window.

So often we assume others know why we do the things we do, why we have the things we have. Unfortunately, most people do not use their psychic ability to figure this out! Having a collection of cats lets people know you like cats, and having German Shepherds lets people know you love German Shepherds. If you have cut crystal, what does that say about you? There is a lot of room for interpretation, so talk about your collections!

Your collections can be a great way for visitors to your home to open up communications with you, finding out more about you. They can also be a wonderful way for friends and family to show you they are thinking about you while they travel or for special occasions.

Tips on Closets Collections and Clutter

From a Feng Shui perspective, we want to keep the space open and clutter free so energy will move easily, but not too swiftly. We want to have order and use common sense. Just because a space was designed for a specific purpose, doesn't mean we have to use it for that purpose if it doesn't serve our needs or wants.

Some suggestions for collections:

Keep them together on one table, in a cabinet, or limit them to one room.

Group them in three's, five' or seven's. Odd numbers seem to work best in most cases.

Put only a few out at a time and rotate them. They lose their importance when you can't see each one easily.

Ask the questions, "How do they feed my soul?" "How much energy do they give me; do they drain me because I have no room for them or because I have to dust them?" "Am I in control here?"

Organizing a clothes closet:

Remove everything. Then as you go through them the first thing to ask is ... Do I love it? Does it make me feel special? Do people comment on how great I look?

If you do love it and you get great compliments on it, try it on. If you don't, get rid of it!

Does it fit? If it's more than one size too small, give it away. If it's too big, put it in a box or bag to take to the alteration store and find out how much it will cost to alter it.

Put like garments together, i.e., blouses, skirts, slacks.

Arrange by color and length.

Organizing a kitchen:

Place cup, dishes, and glasses near the dish washer/ kitchen sink.

Put the spices and baking items close to the stove and oven.

Arrange the pots, pans, casserole dishes and baking sheets near the stove and oven.

Minimize the amounts of pots and pans you have on display, especially hanging over kitchen islands

Put silverware close to the dishes and cooking utensils close to the bake/cook center.

DO NOT display your knives. Put ALL sharp things away in draws.

Store your "holiday items" in the back of corner units, on the top shelf that you can't reach easily, or in the pantry if you have one.

Display your decorative pots, pans, baskets and pottery above the cupboards (if you have a cathedral ceiling or open space above them), hang them on the walls, or display them in various parts of the house.

Put dry goods in air tight containers to prevent pest infestations, boxing like items together in bigger boxes, i.e., packages of beans, rice, pastas, crackers, cereals.

Arrange canned goods, teas/coffees, soups, vegetables, fruits condiments, etc. according to the regularity of use. You may change this seasonally, i.e., soups in front during winter then moved toward the back in summer while mustard, salad dressings and olives get moved forward.

Vitamins, minerals, and nutrition supplements should be put in a separate cupboard away from other food products since their smells can make them taste less than desirable.

Flour, sugar, baking mix products, and cereals stored in large airtight containers in the upper part of cabinet shelves since they are generally used less often and can be seen easier.

Kitchen recipes, warranties, holiday ideas filed in a drawer.

Cleaning products get stored away from food products in their own baskets – have kitchen scouring products in one, bath in another, and living areas in still another.

Recyclable products get their own space.

Put pet supplies next to feeding areas or cleaning areas.

Five questions to organizing linens:

1) *Can you put table linens close to the dining room?*

2) *Is there a draw in the kitchen where dish towels and pot holders can be put?*

3) *Do you have room in your bedroom for you bed linens?*

4) *Is there a large shelf some place where you can store extra pillows and blankets?*

5) *Can the towels for the dogs go in the "doggie wash room" or hung close to the door to dry the animal before it comes inside on rainy days?*

Clutter tips:

1) Please work at keeping the space behind doors clear of items. Doors have to do with the flow of chí, or life. When a door is designed to open 180 degrees, but you have so much stuff behind it so it will only open 90 degrees, the subconscious tells you are limiting the flow of "good chí" by 50%. We do not want to do this.

2) Visually, the over-the-door hangers give you the impression you don't have enough room, a sense of "lack" of room. This "lack" mentality can create a lack in the good things

of life. Again we want to work at eliminating these whenever possible.

3) Doors that don't close completely mean we don't follow through on the physical plane with our creative ideas. We want to be able to "open" new opportunities and "close", or finish, existing projects.

4) If clutter gathers in the two or more locations of the same area of life, when using the Ba-gua as a guide to these areas, there may be an emotional blockage occurring. Consider seeking professional advice; i.e., **partnership** area, speak to a therapist or spiritual counselor, **wealth** area, speak to a financial planner or CPA.

5) Clutter on the desk suggests you are lacking in time or organizational skills, that you don't value yourself and your space.

6) Tall book shelves filled with books behind your desk can overpower you, make you feel uncomfortable, and add stress to your life.

7) Keeping things from your past can keep you in the past. When sorting through boxes of items you have inherited, ask yourself what emotion do I feel when I see this? Keep only those things that "light your fire"! You want joy to emanate from as many memories of the past as possible.

8) Hoarding "stuff" stops the flow — the circulation — of life. By releasing items, you are allowing the circulation to begin again. This can apply to money, career, hopes and dreams. All areas of life are affected by the "stoppage" in one area and, alternately, improved by clearing energy in any area.

9) Sometimes having too many books will give you a feeling of inadequacy, low self-esteem. Look at the number of books you have. Go through them and ask when was the last time I used it? Do I have space for it? Could you get rid of this book and find the information some other way?

Nine Steps to Organization,
by Anacaria Myrrha

Attitudes

1. Time. To Begin, you must be willing to commit the necessary time and attention to set up the systems. However many hours it takes, this investment will save you hundreds of hours (and a lot of anxiety) in the future. How long it takes will depend on the size of the task and the number of hours you can devote on any given day. Basic paper and workflow systems can usually be set up in a day, small filing systems in a week, large filing systems take longer. Projects, like photo albums or travel files, can be gathered in boxes and worked on one at a time, a method that helps defuse the sense of overwhelm. Once a system is in use, refinements and modifications can be made as necessary.

2. Decisions. Next, you must be willing to make the necessary decisions to set up the systems. If you turn the design over to someone else, you will wind up with a system that works for them but not necessarily for you. Your systems need to be created with attention to your particular priorities, patterns and style.

3. Change. You must also be willing to embrace new habits. If you find yourself saying, "That's the way I've always done it," or, "I've always been disorganized, unfocused, late..." try a new approach. Begin to say, "I used to be disorganized, unfocused and late, but now I'm organized, focused, and on time." Positive speaking, like positive thinking, is a very powerful tool and can be used to your advantage. With this approach, and the support of systems designed with ease of use as a factor, the transition to new habits can be easy.

4. Maintenance. Because being organized is a process and not a goal, you must be willing to commit regular time to maintain your systems. This is the one we often put off because we are taking care of what seem to be more urgent tasks. However, when chaos piles up, the simplest tasks become difficult and time consuming as we search for bills to pay or our child's school authorization form. With the constant flow of information and paper in our lives, and our changing personal and professional needs, it is crucial to schedule regular time to plan, to file, and to update systems.

Components of Organization

5. Containers. One reason disorder occurs is the lack of boundaries. Without boundaries, paper piles spill onto other paper piles. Pens and pencils, rubber bands and paper clips become a jumble in desk drawers. Children's toys, kitchen utensils, tools and hardware become mixed together and are time consuming and annoying to retrieve. A container is the first step in the solution. A container sets limits on the space the items inhabit and keeps them in their place.

Containers come in all shapes and sizes. File folders, file cabinets and desk racks contain papers. Drawers and drawer organizers contain tools. Planning notebooks contain appointments, tasks and resources. Even an increment of time can be viewed as a container (a task scheduled from 1:00 to 3:00 on Tuesday afternoon can be comfortably set aside until its time arrives). Magazine boxes and shelves, scrapbooks and photo albums all act as containers to set boundaries for objects and information, and help to create order in our lives.

6. Labels. The second component is the right label on a container. This label tells you (and others) what belongs in the container. More important, it tells you (and others) what does not belong in the container.

7. Procedures. A procedure should be thought out for getting things into and out of each container. If the procedure has several steps, it can be written down on a card and attached to the container. For instance the procedures for filing health insurance claims can be taped to the front of a vertical file rack containing file folders of claims in their various stages of completion.

8. Location. If you have old IRS records in your desk drawers and resource information for a current project in a file cabinet with your ski equipment stacked in front of it, your project work will be difficult and your anxiety level high. Put the IRS records in labeled, uniform-size storage boxes in the closet and ban the skis to the garage. Place your Current Projects and Action Files in a desk file drawer or in a vertical rack on your work surface. Also, keep all the necessary tools for particular tasks in the area where the work is done.

Asking for Help

9. The Professional Organizer. Most of us have mechanics to doctor our cars, accountants to prepare our tax returns, lawyers to negotiate our contracts and housekeepers to tidy our nests. However, it is often difficult for us to ask for help with a task about which we feel out of control, embarrassed, or that we ought to be able to do ourselves. Remember, being organized is not a moral issue. It is a skill that can be learned. The good news is, help is available. You can now hire a professional organizer to help you learn that skill. A professional organizer can offer creative problem solving and an objective view, provide you with practical solutions, and support you and keep you on track during the process of change.

* * * * * * * *

Going through a closet to keep only the things you love and use can be one of the greatest gifts you can give yourself. It reminds you how special you are, that you have beautiful things and beautiful memories. Do you need to keep the things or are the memories enough? Only you can answer that.

Collections bring us joy by reminding us of how we acquired each piece. They share with others who we are and what matters to us in this world. Finding a way to create a sense of balance between collections and clutter is a challenge we will probably continue to have the rest of our lives.

We go through different cycles in each day, week, month, and year. Sometimes we NEED the item. That's OK I still have things belonging to my loved ones. I also have released many.

When we release an item there is a void — a space left open where once it was filled, a vacuum. It is said that the Universe abhors a vacuum. It wants to fill it! When you get rid of something, you are creating a vacuum and the Universe wants to fill it for you. It could be with more STUFF or it could be with more TIME — time to be alone, time to be with loved ones, time you can use to create the dreams of your life, or the "Life of Your Dreams", your choice. I suggest you go for balance.

Contact Information:

Anacaria Myrrha, Simple Systems, San Rafael, California

National Association of Professional Organizers (NAPO) National Headquarters, 512-454-8626

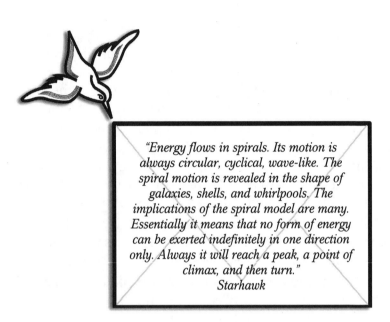

"Energy flows in spirals. Its motion is always circular, cyclical, wave-like. The spiral motion is revealed in the shape of galaxies, shells, and whirlpools. The implications of the spiral model are many. Essentially it means that no form of energy can be exerted indefinitely in one direction only. Always it will reach a peak, a point of climax, and then turn."
Starhawk

Healing Environments

To those who aspire to a lifetime in the garden –
May it surround you with beauty and joy,
May it teach you its songs.
To the garden –
May you surround us with your beauty, your joy
and your
universal language of earth, sun, water and seed.
May you teach us your songs!
author unknown

I knew what healing environments looked like long before I started to study interior design and Feng Shui, and so do you. I am not talking about hospitals and other health care facilities, but the places we gravitate to which heal not just the body – they include the healing of the mind and spirit as well. Many medical facilities could benefit from our inner knowing.

Until the time our medical profession and insurance companies discover how many people they can heal and keep well through the creation of proper environments for healing, we must take it upon ourselves to design them into our own homes. We can become aware of the exterior "healing" properties used in good design that will fill the human needs within the facilities. Let me explain what I mean by clarifying some of the terms I am using.

What I am referring to when I say "exterior healing properties used in good design," are things like the color chosen for the project. For instance, we know through research and studies the color pink is a very relaxing color, a color associated with love.

When I say, "fill the human needs within the facilities," my reference is to the qualities a human being needs at the time of medical services which might be called an extension of "good bedside manners". It's more than just a kind touch, and a sincere listening ear, (which is called "active listening"). It's the warm blanket when you are cold and the pillow under you legs when you have to lie flat on your back.

If we are experiencing a health challenge, every part of us is in need of healing – our body, mind and spirit. The medical community may be brought in to facilitate with the process to help the body. The mind and spirit can be helped through properties considered "Good Feng Shui". These properties include light, color, sound, living objects and other life-affirming energies.

People from all cultures and walks of life know this on some level, but we often forget when a crisis hits. Having flowers at the gift shop of hospitals is a gentle reminder for us to get out of our heads – our mental thinking – and connect with our hearts – the center of love. In fact, it is said that a Bonsai plant is the best possible gift to give someone who is experiencing a depletion of vital energy because it is a total "living" unit – a vital living plant which often contains a small human figure, fish and other elements of the natural world.

I love to tell stories about my personal experiences because it allows you to understand what I'm trying to teach. Writing this book is a way to connect with another human being in a written form and sharing my experiences, my stories. Often it's the way the story imparts the message, making an impact on the emotions that helps you remember the important information which is needed at some later point.

Many years ago I experienced a serious health challenge where I lost a great deal of blood. My doctor performed surgery, then left on a planned vacation thinking everything was progressing normally. On the fourth day a nurse inquired if they had done a blood test to see how much blood I had lost. I had no idea if a test had been performed, so she investigated. They had not.

When they received the results, they immediately ordered four units of blood for a transfusion. This was in the early years of the HIV virus. They stated the tests were accurate with nothing to worry about. So they prepared to start the procedure.

A couple of curious things occurred at this point. First, my mother, who was suppose to be working, showed up at the hospital. When I asked her why she had come, her reply surprised me. "I just felt I needed to be here today. Even though you are in your mid-thirties, you will always be my little girl." I was touched by the sentiment and then explained that they were about to do this transfusion.

The second occurred about 15 minutes later when I started to have a severe reaction to the transfusion. So severe was the reaction that I could not call the nurse, My mother who was sitting in the room had to get help. To this day we do not know what caused it, but it created enough doubt in my mind to make me choose a different solution. Instead of following the logical medical advice, I used a hidden gift called intuition.

My intuition, supported by the feminine energy of my mother's intuition, gave me the courage to say no to the remainder of the process. I was warned that my decision was stupid, that it would take me many months or even a year or more to recover, but I stayed with the decision. For the first time in my life I made a conscious decision regarding my own health and well-being.

A few months later it was discovered that the tests for the HIV virus they were using at the time were not as accurate as they thought. Several of the hospitals, including the one I had attended, had received tainted blood. I will share with you right now, I am lucky. No trace of the virus has shown up in the blood tests through all these years.

What were the chances of my mother taking the day off work, and arriving just 15 minutes before the reaction to the transfusion? What made me question the continuance of the treatment? I do not have any way to prove it, but I feel it was a Higher Power guiding all of us.

I went home knowing it was going to be a long recovery time. I would sleep all but two or three hours a day, just getting up to fix meals for the family. I did not like to be in my bedroom. I found it to be very cold and very uncomfortable.

I had a couple of favorite spots. One looked out the window down into the creek at the base of the house where tall oak trees grew. The other looked out into the back yard where the pool was located. I could look at the ducks flying in and swimming around. Both rooms held lots of good memories and had colors that nurtured me. As I got better, I would walk outside and sit by the side of the pool and later in my recovery, by the creek that was down a hill. This meant I had to climb back up. It felt like climbing a mountain because I was so weak. I used this walk back up our driveway as a measurement of my progress in gaining strength – my progress in healing.

Years later I discovered water is the element of the feminine, an essential healing element for all, and especially for a woman. It is said it is especially useful on the emotional level.

Views of nature are healing, connecting us to the Source of our life, the Great Creator. Being in rooms filled with wonderful memories support our spirit. Rooms filled with light, warm our soul. Watching the ducks in flight lifted my spirit. Walking down the path to the creek led me to contemplate the journey of life.

The colors of the rooms correlated to the frequencies I needed to aid in the healing of my injuries. Color is a powerful tool in our lives. There is so much that we know about them and I feel there is so much we don't know. We know they have their own frequencies just like the musical notes of a scale. I know the room I spent most of my time in contained a majority of orange, (it was the late 70's, early 80's), and according to the chakra system of colors, orange relates to the 2nd chakra.

The chakras are believed to be energy centers located within the human body. Depending on the source of information and what you are doing with it, there can be seven or more centers. For simplicity, we will say there are seven centers. Starting at the base of the spine and moving upward you start with the color red. Then you move up the body in the order of the rainbow.

So the first chakra is the base chakra with the color red. The 2nd chakra is the sacral area with the color orange, followed by the 3rd chakra in the region of the belly button with the color yellow. The 4th chakra is the in the area of the heart with the color green. Blue is the color for the throat chakra, and

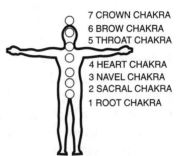

7 CROWN CHAKRA
6 BROW CHAKRA
5 THROAT CHAKRA

4 HEART CHAKRA
3 NAVEL CHAKRA
2 SACRAL CHAKRA
1 ROOT CHAKRA

that is the 5th one. The space above the brow on the forehead is considered the brow chakra, or third eye, and has the color that is associated with indigo. The 7th chakra's color is purple and is known as the crown chakra.

I have included a list for you along with other related information on colors at the end of this chapter.

There was a very famous interior designer, Tony Torrice, ASID, who worked with disabled children. He told stories regarding the chakra centers and how they relate to the disability of the child. I share stories in my classes about the results he gathered. Unfortunately, Tony died before I could share with him one of my favorite stories. It was about Jeff, my son, choosing to wear a purple beanie after his brain surgery.

My surgery was abdominal in nature. Being in a room with orange was probably the best color I could have surrounded myself with.

I was still recovering when my mother became ill. As I shared earlier, I had to find a place for her to live. The first "home" I found was what they call a retirement inn. It had great places for the residents to gather, water around the grounds, floral wallpaper, lots of windows and skylights, and friendly people. They traveled on trips and in many ways I wanted to live there myself.

Less than two months later, they told me my mother had to leave. Her disease had progressed so quickly we needed to find a convalescent home. I looked and looked and looked. I went all over Santa Clara Valley to find one where I could feel comfortable . . . comfortable enough to visit and comfortable enough to leave Mom there. They were horrible places – dark, dirty, institutional. The people in them were the same – negative, disheveled, cold. I did not know what to do.

I finally found one. It was light, open, airy. There was a fountain in the court yard, and most of the rooms looked out onto it. EVERY room had a window. There were beautiful pictures on the wall and the furniture looked as though it had come from a model home – beautiful, clean, soft, inviting. There was wallpaper on most of the walls and molding around the doors and ceiling. There was even wainscoting in some areas.

The people reflected the same open, light-hearted, home-caring attitude of the surroundings they worked in. We were allowed to personalize the room. I brought in art she had at home, her favorite "toys" for the grandchildren, and pictures of her loved ones. There were cats and dogs in the neighborhood who came to visit occasionally. When the children who owned them came, there was laughter, giggles, hugs and kisses. Birthdays were celebrated with cake and ice cream and movies with popcorn provided. There was a radiance of light that emanated from this convalescent "home". There was hope and love and healing.

Mom could not recover from this disease she had, it is the same as Mad Cow's Disease. She died a few months later, but I knew she had been very happy in this place – the last of her homes.

Through these stories you have "heard, seen, felt, smelled and tasted" what is needed in a healing environment. We innately know it. We get busy, too busy to care for our body, mind and spirit. We do not even trust the feeling in our gut.

Let me share one last story. It has to do with trusting our own "knowingness".

I have always loved to look at houses, inside and out. I

would go to open houses, model homes, and showcase mansions from the time I was in grammar school. My grandmother taught me how to sew when I was seven and I often helped her make curtains and draperies for her clients. I studied the details of woodworking because I was intrigued with the craftsmanship. I have always created with my hands.

At one point we had a financial opportunity that would allow us to move into the house I described earlier. I had seen this house some weeks before from the outside. It was intriguing to me. That weekend it was open for viewing. My first feeling inside was of warmth – it had a fire going in the fireplace. Beyond that, I didn't care for most of it. It was dark and cold and something haunted me.

But my husband loved it and wanted it. Through much effort we bought it. Of all the properties we had ever bought or sold, this was the most challenging. I especially disliked the master bedroom and bathroom plus there was one small bedroom that was dark and foreboding.

This house, although a very lovely house as we remodeled it, was a place of much sadness for me personally. I was often sick in this house, had my mother and son die while living here, and went through a divorce here as well.

Many years after I had moved from this house, I learned several other families who have lived there had similar experiences. From a Feng Shui perspective, many Asians will not buy a home of sadness believing that a house of misfortune will continue to be a house of misfortune for all who live there.

Being aware of the feelings you have regarding your environment and taking appropriate action to support them is very important. I mentioned the aspect of my discomfort regarding the master bedroom for a purpose. As with several other parts of this chapter, it has to do with color, our response to color and our emotional feelings.

Several years ago I did some work with an associate of

Jacob Liberman, author of "Light, Medicine of the Future". We were measuring my response to different color light for use in therapy work. Since I have been fascinated with the responses invoked by light within the human being for decades, I was ecstatic to be able to participate.

While going through the process, we discovered I should work with the color "lime green" as it had the strongest response. Now let me tell you, although I like green, it is not lime green that I like. I prefer blue-green. I agreed to continue with the testing.

Week after week I sat in front of this flashing "lime green" light. I could make it go faster, or slower, sitting there about half an hour each time.

One day I came in totally depressed. My energy level had been dropping over the last few weeks, but I never associated it with the color therapy. That day I had the horrifying experience of re-living a date rape. I had never connected the facts of 1) the clothing I was wearing and 2) the room I was in to the color **lime green.** It was an intense reaction. I am so grateful for the experience and my therapist who help me through the experience.

Why do I share this with you? Because the carpet in the master bedroom was "lime green". I never liked it from the moment I saw it, wanting to tear it out, but it was the only "new" carpet put in the house. We had so many other ideas and projects it seemed ridiculous to remove something that was "functional" at that point. I also intensely disliked the wallpaper for the same reason, plus the fact the pattern had not been matched when it was installed constantly bothered me.

The quality of the work, or craftsmanship, within the home plays a major role as well. The time and energy put into the creation of the accessories, furniture and even maintenance of the home make a difference in the healing qualities of your dwellings. I will discuss maintenance and cleaning later.

Furniture styles impart energy which can aid or drain

energy, especially in healing. Some styles create a sense of imbalance, as though they will fall over. Others might be very sharp like a knife, possibly cutting you, or just make you feel uncomfortable because of their pointedness. You get a real good feel of this when you are in hospitals and medical facilities.

Have you noticed how many sharp objects there are in hospitals? Think of all the instruments, wires, tubes, and machines they have. How do you "feel" around them? While it is true we need them, they are artificial objects that separate the human body from that which is natural. Even the long, straight corridors can drain you of energy. They are called "Killer Chí" in China.

Everything in our environment affects us on one level or another. We can become paranoid and immobilized if we are not careful, worrying whether we are doing the right thing. This book is here as a guide to awaken your awareness of your surroundings – inside the home and office and all around you.

Trust yourself in your ability to make the right decisions for yourself and your loved ones. As you work with this knowledge you become more "in tune" with the energies around you, you pick up the frequencies just like an antenna. You will know if there is a transmission of negative stuff coming toward you so you can get out of the way. And you can choose to be in the presence of gentle, joyful, life-giving energy.

Many tools can be used to aid in the healing of the physical, mental, emotional and spiritual bodies. Areas of research include lighting, plants, sound/music, bringing in living animals (dogs and cats), attracting animals (bird baths, hummingbird and squirrel feeders), touch, color, hypnotherapy, softening institutional look, prayers, positive thinking, affirmations, herbs and aromatherapy, gardens, water (both flowing and in ponds), labyrinths, crystals and rocks, laughter and humor, visual goals, support groups, pictures of loved ones, landscapes and life-affirming pictures plus travel and vacation posters.

Each person is different. Plus we go through many different cycles of life. Refer to the lists of questions presented toward the beginning of this book. What was your nurturing spot like as a child? Have you recreated it or parts of it in your home? Have you learned what a nurturing spot looks like to your loved ones? Is that represented in your dwelling? If not, it's time to start. If you have, good for you!

Not only do objects impact our healing, the height of ceilings will also affect us. Sometimes we need the low ceiling with a darkish room for "licking our wounds" or going inward to discover a deeper part of our being. Other times we need to be inspired by high cathedral ceilings and lots of light. This is why most religious buildings provide us with both.

Your cultural heritage is important to consider and incorporate also. Many of these suggestions are universal, transcending cultures. If you have a particular "ritual" from your spiritual, religious, or cultural background, embody it. We are our past. Embrace it! Find a way that works for you in your life.

Our spirits, our souls, our bodies, our minds, all will need to be healed at various points in our lives. Our home may be the only place we are physically able to do this. Bring in the love of your God, the Highest Good, to keep watch over you, to surround you, to protect you and to watch over you and empower you through the calling of Its Creations into your home.

Evaluating Your Environment

> "Creativity is inventing,
> experimenting, growing,
> taking risks, breaking rules,
> making mistakes,
> and having fun."
> Mary Lou Cook

Our environment gives us a multitude of energy – from the energy we receive from sleeping and eating to the energy of family and friends. We also receive energy from the objects we own. Pictures remind us of loved ones and good times with family. There can also be the negative energy of a poor choice of furniture which can crack the foundation of our self-confidence.

It is very important for us to surround ourselves with things we love and that inspire us. If we have things that "eat away" at the beauty of our soul and spirit, then they "eat away" at the essence of our home. The following are some questions for you to consider as you become aware of the objects in and around your dwelling.

Do a mental inventory of the furniture in your house.

Do you love it?

How did you get it? Bought it at a store? At a yard sale? Given to me?

If used, do you know the people? What kind of energy did they have when they owned it? Getting divorced? Loving? Gentle?

Do a physical inventory of your artwork and accessories?

How many pictures do you have? Sculptures? Accessories?

How many:
Inspire
Motivate
Are life-affirming
Show scarcity/lack
Prosperity/Abundance
Show cycles of life
Build team work
Build and support relationships
Develop individuality and independence
Are sacred or Holy
Represent spirituality
Have living plants or animals
Show families, friends or communities
Evoke sadness
Give encouragement
Bring in other cultures
Were created by friends
Build faith
Depict anger
Are of nature
Are calm and peaceful
Depict helpfulness
Express protection
Express love
Show activity
Express health
Encourage helping people
Give a sense of intelligence or genius
Are healing

Thoughts on Color

"*Energy is
eternal delight.*"
William Blake

The Chakra System

Purple:Seventh Chakra
Connects us to our spiritual self
Wealth (abundance)
Inspirational – Highest human ideals
Indigo: Sixth Chakra
Connects us to our unconscious self
The "Third Eye"
Intuition - Meditation
Blue: Fifth Chakra
Connects us to holistic thought
Knowledge
Movement toward spiritual awareness
Green: Fourth Chakra
Connects us to unconditional love
Wood - New life
Family (tree)
Yellow: Third Chakra
Connects us to mental self
Earth
Health
Orange: Second Chakra
Connects us to emotional self
Feelings
Red: First Chakra
Connects us to physical self
Activating color (To stimulate or create balance)
Fame
Fire

"*To be really great in little things,
to be truly noble and heroic in the
insipid details of everyday life, is a
virtue so rare as to be worthy of
cannonization.*"
Harriet Beecher Stowe

Symbology of Cleaning and Maintenance

Cleaning up your own stuff: the joy and accomplishment.

Myths and stories are a way to transcend cultural barriers and to learn from other people's experiences. Mythology was one of my favorite subjects in school and has led me on many a journey into new fields of knowledge. Similar stories told in different cultures will have the same meaning. I find this fascinating.

Other than visits to the Chinatowns of Los Angeles and San Francisco, interior design was my first introduction to the Chinese culture. I loved the intricate carvings, the bright red and gold they decorated with, and the stories I heard about their land. The mystical dragon has lured me into many a tale, including Feng Shui. The symbology in the landscape intrigued me, my "little child" was filled with joy and wonder.

When I discovered there was even more symbology in houses, my "little kid" jumped with joy. It was the mythology and symbology that turned this foreign philosophy into a form of play. I discovered my clients loved it also. When I heard this next story on cultural traditions, I stopped to think how wonderful it would be for our culture to adopt parts of it.

As the Chinese New Year approaches, many things are prepared for the celebration. One that most people have heard of is the costume for the Dragon Parade. Inside most businesses they prepare an altar to feed Buddha as well and give him gifts. They will put out tangerines, sand, water, flowers and firecrackers to name a few of the gifts. They do this because they want to attract good chí to their business for the New Year by attracting good chí to Buddha.

To bring Good Luck into the home for the New Year, the first thing they do is clean the house. They do not want anything old, worn-out, or negative in the house because that would attract more of the same type of energy or chí into the house. They will clean the entire house, pay all the bills, and clean the refrigerator. They will buy new staples – flour, sugar, rice and tea – to bring in fresh energy, new possibilities and the hope the New Year has to offer. They do this to please Buddha, their Higher Power.

What a concept! Clean out the old to make way for the new! Clean the house to greet the New Year. Remove the boxes and wrapping paper. Remove a dead tree. Get rid of the leftovers, and pay off all debts.

Wouldn't that be a great way to start the new year? Would that make you feel great? Would starting the year debt free make a world of difference to you? It sure would for me!

Many years later I was able to do just that. Seeing space in the refrigerator, knowing all bills, except the mortgage, had been paid off, and having a zero balance on the credit cards was incredibly freeing. I felt lighter, as though a weight had been lifted from my shoulders. I bought fresh flowers and plants to greet the New Year with beauty, grace, joy and love.

Soon I realized the power behind this. Not only was I clearing the space of "negative" energy, I was calling in the good energy of my Higher Power. I was creating a ceremony around the cleaning of my house. I knew I loved the freshness and sparkle of the furniture and glass, but before, I did not like to work at it.

What I found was this: if I focused my attention on cleaning with the intention of making more room for God to be present in my life, the cleaning went quicker and more easily. There was a shift in energy that everyone could feel. There was a sense of pride, in me and in the home. Everyone benefited from this energy. For what happens to us affects everyone and everything around us.

I started to share this with family and friends. Many found it fascinating and decided to try it themselves. I suggested several ideas to help them create rituals for their own homes, to fill specific needs or desires. We discovered the more attention we put into the concept of a Higher Power helping us through this, the more fun we had. It became play rather than work.

Other discoveries occurred. I found decorating doorways helped me with communications, it flowed more easily. Cleaning windows helped me see my dreams more clearly, so I could focus on the possibilities. Making room in attics helped raise my awareness of a Higher Power present in my life, watching over me. Clearing the basement released old negative beliefs and patterns from my subconscious that were holding me down. These discoveries became the basis for my Simply Sacred Space classes.

I found many people are not aware of the simple things they do everyday and the impact it has on their subconscious. This results in more work and less play in their lives. For instance, the simple act of completely closing a drawer. By not closing it, the subconscious grasps the incompletion. You do not have enough time to complete simple things, so why complete major things? By simply following through with the closing of the drawer you will find, more gets complete in your life.

Symbology in the home helps us to relate to our homes. Our subconscious is calling to us, asking us to help it grow. It relates to our body and our body relates to our home. There are hidden meanings in everything. Here are a few of them.

1) *Living plants give us the oxygen we need to live, so they represent the breath of life, growth and vitality.*

2) *Lights and candles represent the light of God within you, your own inner beauty. Let it shine brightly by cleaning them regularly. They also bring in warmth and the fire element.*

3) *Mirrors reflect who you are while windows are your eyes, your vision. Both are windows to the soul. You want to be seen "clearly" by everyone so make sure they are clean and not cracked. Repair or replace them if they are. Looking in the mirror everyday, speaking affirmations to yourself, will change your life in a positive fashion.*

4) *Wind is the breath of life and the winds of change. Life is always changing and moving. Have something that reminds you on a subconscious level to "get on with life" so you do not get "stuck in a rut".*

5) *Open floor plans have no boundaries and relate to lack of boundaries in life. Use area rugs to "set" boundaries in life.*

6) *Hot tubs, hot water heaters and washing machines seem to create "hot water" experiences. Change the thought to one of releasing the old, washing it away.*

7) *Molds and mildews are associated with growths of unwanted things, besides the fact many people are allergic to them.*

8) *Cracked foundations and "dry rot" relate to your stability in life.*

9) *Partial walls can create an imbalance where the physical body is out of alignment with your spiritual mind. This sometimes shows up in lots of wonderful ideas that are never even attempted.*

Simple maintenance of the house can have major impacts on our lives. I gave the front door a new coat of paint and polished the front door handle one weekend. It's in the career area of the house. All four of us are self-employed. We all had several new clients come to us in the next few weeks. Opportunity knocks. Will you open the door?

Listen to the words you use. They give clues to the areas of your house you can change to create the life you want to live. I have "fixed" many fax machines and computers that were repeatedly breaking down because other people were looking at a "doom and gloom", "if-anything-can-go-wrong-it-will" Murphy's Law. Remove the law, change the visual message we are programming it, and watch the change!

I take many pictures to show in my classes. It has helped me to become more "focused" on the details in life. There is a saying that if you take care of the details, the rest of life will take care of itself. This is especially true in the kitchen.

Pay attention to how you clean the stove, and pay attention to what you are thinking about while preparing meals. Would it feel better to hang all the pots and pans, or maybe just a few and put the rest out of sight? Are you cooking with a good attitude or do you hate cooking and let everyone know it? Which attitude would create a good tasting meal?

Learn more about the messages your house is giving you. Listen to you inner voice. It will tell you what needs to be fixed right away and what can wait. Listen . . . it's whispering to you. Do you hear it?

"There is a spirit and a need and a man at the beginning of every great human advance. Every one of these must be right for that particular moment of history, or nothing happens."
Coretta Scott King

Furniture, Accessories and Energy

> "Spirit is the real and eternal;
> matter is the unreal and
> temporal."
> Mary Baker Eddy

Long ago I heard a story about furniture possessing energy – energy of the rooms they have been in, energy of the occupants who have been in the rooms and energy of the materials they were made from. It was almost thirty years ago when a well-known designer who was teaching the class made this statement. Her comment went something like this:

> "You need to clean the energy of antique furniture from the Victorian era since it can create restrictions and limitations on one's love life when it is placed in your bedroom."

She continued to explain the mentality surrounding women in those days and how it could negatively affect a woman's worth.

My suggestion of a way to do that is to light a candle and bless the furniture.

Obviously, it made an impact on me otherwise I wouldn't remember it today. I thought she was a bit crazy, but it was food for thought. It had another affect on me as well, for I decided not to have any Victorian furniture in my life. I did not need to co-mingle with that type of energy.

I totally forgot this story until I started consciously working with the energies in and around the environment. Developing a person's living space requires an exchange of energy between the designer and the client. Master bedrooms are a private, sacred space for the partners living there. The furniture in these rooms radiate the emotions of their lives. I could feel this. I could sense when it was filled with love and when love was missing.

One day I walked into a room and felt overpowered by energy from the past, many people and emotions. I was "staging" the house for a Realtor to help him sell it, making it look appealing to potential buyers. It was filled with grief, hatred, abuse, anger, the energy of many generations in the house – parents, grandparents, and four children. I told him what I was experiencing and made suggestions to change it. The look on his face told me long before the words came out of his mouth that my "sensing" was correct.

Animal energy is very important to our existence. We are connected to them on levels we have long forgotten. When we relied on our instincts to provide us with food, we could sense their presence. Several hunters I know say they connect with the environment when they hunt. They strive to become one with the landscape, plants and animals, so there is no distinction between them. They become aware of **all surrounding** living energy – trees, shrubs, animals, land forms.

Native Americans honored the animals. They would never kill an animal just for the sport of it. It would be asked of the Great Spirit to provide an animal and bless it before presenting itself to be killed for food and clothing.

Animals represent or are symbolic of certain energies. They are signs or give signals of energies to look for and be aware of. Walking in the wilderness areas you discover this. As you become more aware of their nature, you will discover when one is acting out of character for its breed. It may be sick or it may need your attention directed toward it.

My experience has shown me that although we may live in the city the animals will get your attention. They do this through photographs, paintings, stuffed animals, notepads, calendars, gift items, T-shirts/sweatshirts, statues, and jewelry. Even the animal names of automobile styles signify their energy.

Ever been drawn to a picture of a dog or wolf? Want to touch the bronze statue of a horse? Do you hear the sound of a dolphin when you see the glass sculpture at the museum? The animal spirit is calling to you. It could be giving you a message, supporting your decision at work or guiding you further along your life's purpose and journey.

I had a raven guide me to a shop where I found a basket I was looking for. I wanted to learn more of the native cultures of the Pacific Northwest when I saw the raven. It flew ahead of me for many miles as I traveled down this certain road. The next time I saw a raven was on a casino sign. When I was in the gift shop looking for information, an artist came in to sell her craft. The shop was not interested, but it was exactly what I was looking for.

A Golden Eagle swooped down to alert me it was time to write this book. It was a message to be heroic, to connect the masculine power of doing (physically sitting and writing) with the healing powers of the Divine Spirit (getting the message of intuition out of my head and into a book for others to learn from). Eagles represent creativity, passion, alchemy of life, and an awakening sense of a Higher Power in healing and spirituality.

I use artwork in many commercial environments to bring in a sense of teamwork or to help creativity. Sometimes it is to help responsible actions to occur, for people to act responsibly.

Toward the back of this book you will find lists of plants and animals with suggestions of some of the energies which might be associated with them. I have also included a list of questions for you regarding the type of artwork you already have. Do you know what the message is it imparts to you? What emotional response do you receive from it? If we have depressing pictures, we can become drained. Joyful or inspirational scenes can enhance our living environments and feed our soul.

Remember, nothing is permanent nor is it always correct. What works for one person may or may not work for another. My **response** to an animal or color is based upon who I am and my experiences of life. You are different. Your experiences are different. Your emotions are different. Your needs are different. And the cycles of life are constantly changing you and your needs.

Explore the possibilities of the energies of your furniture – the wood and materials they are made from, and the energy of the craftsperson who designed it. Through the discovery of the energies of your accessories you can bring in additional opportunities to enrich your life. This is one of the many gifts your dwellings can give you.

Homes of the Future

What is becoming clear in our society is the need with which we approach the shelters we are building. We have government organizations and regulations that have legal guidelines called building codes. Research is being conducted to study the responses of exterior influences on the health of human beings. Other factors like the amount of available land, building costs, and the need for the various functions within the house create a challenge for the home improvement industry. We are going to have to work with all of these in some cases. What else might we need to look at?

In the 1950's, the home was one's castle and the most telling symbol of upward mobility. Forty years later the home has become a metaphor for societal evolution. It combines the needs to work, raise children, care for aging parents, seek refuge and express individuality. Function has overcome form. Above all, home has become a kind of expression of personal creativity. It has to have our look and it must be organized. Furnishings have to be comfortable and easy to care for plus have more flexibility in their uses. We want "feel, function and convenience".

Homes of the future will need to incorporate many areas of design that are usually dealt with on a one-at-a-time basis only. These areas include:

1) *barrier free design,*
2) *eldercare needs,*
3) *green design, management of remodeling wastes and wise utilization of natural resources,*
4) *air quality using EPA standards,*
5) *incorporating the needs for disabilities such as hearing and sight impaired,*
6) *increased occupancy challenges caused by expanded "family-of-choice," and mutli-generational cultural traditions,*
7) *energy efficiency, passive solar, and seasonal landscaping,*
8) *Feng Shui,*
9) *traditional design and detailing.*

Many things are happening in the world today that are drastically changing the way the future is going to be. We have modern technology so we can view events as they occur throughout the world. We are living longer, healthier lives due to modern technology. In addition, things that can possibly harm us in different ways are becoming more well known. For instance, we now know about air quality for our lungs, psychotherapy for our emotional behavior, and ergonomics for our bodies, all of which are relatively new.

Looking at each of these areas in greater detail shows a trend toward improved quality of living for more people.

People with disabilities involving their legs often wind up in wheel chairs, their minds and the rest of their body functioning well. In fact, very often they are gifted in other areas. Yet most homes are designed without giving any thought to this fact. Barrier free and wheelchair accessible design can be beautiful, often offering great solutions for use by children.

I heard a speaker say several years ago that through modern medical technology, the life expectancy has increased by 15 years over what our grandparents could expect. Yet society only sees that we can work until we are 62 to 65 years of age. "Vitalaging" is now a verb meaning "living life fully into your 80's and 90's". Sometimes the body is not able to function well at that age, but homes need to be designed safely to allow the elderly a long and productive life, fully supported in this by their living environment.

The alternative to cutting down trees to build new houses needs to be addressed. In some cases, steel 2 x 4's can be used for the support studs. Other locations in the country might be able to use straw bales, rubber tires, or create earth domes. Discarded construction materials account for nearly 70% of our landfill! According to Karol Dewulf Nickells, editor-in-chief of Traditional Home Magazine, more money will be spent on remodeling construction than on new construction in the coming years. That is why they have targeted a new magazine just for that market.

We now know that many health challenges associated with the lungs can be tied to people's environments. It can be their type of work, air quality in the home, or something from the out-of-doors such as smog. The October 1995 issue of Better Homes and Gardens Magazine showed "Health House '95", a remodeled house that was cosponsored by the magazine and the American Lung Association in Minneapolis. Being a remodel, there were limitations, but it gave many great ideas on how to improve the home for better, more healthful living in the 21st Century.

Disabilities come in many forms. As we continue to live longer and grow technologically, we have learned that hearing and sight-impaired individuals can live very productive lives if given the right tools to work with. Lighting, color, flooring and texture can make a space beautiful, but can cause challenges for some people with disabilities. Again, this often is an overlooked area in home design.

Another speaker I heard several years ago shared this interesting information.

Housing as we have seen it in the past will be changing. Starting in 1996, every 7.5 minutes another baby boomer will turn 50 years old. Those of us who will admit to being a baby boomer are called the "sandwich generation". Sandwiched between when our children leave home and our elderly parents need our attention. We have children who cannot afford housing because their starting salaries are half what the starting salaries were 20 years ago for the same position with the same degree. Most children will live at home until they are 30 years old while attending college and getting started.

Our parents were forced to retire at 65 leaving them financially and emotionally drained. Now, they are more frail and it is necessary to look after them. It takes two incomes to afford a home in the San Francisco Bay Area, often leaving little time for quality family life and the question arises, "who will be home to take care of Dad, of Mom?"

Designing homes for the future, which is now.

Homes need to be designed to accommodate multi-generations, whether they be for birth families or "families-of-choice". Many different cultures immigrating here also believe in having many generations living under one roof. These new demands require privacy and common areas with flexibility. A home may need to accommodate three generations and a home office. It may need room for two generations, a nanny, and a home office. With the investment in remodeling costs being so large, people need to look at the long term prospect of resale or a logical way for several families to co-own and feel good about their investment.

We have known about solar energy for years and there are many beautiful designs that can be included in home design. Other things to consider are natural air-conditioning systems, drought resistant landscaping, and proper placement of plants to maximize solar efficiency.

With the increase of Asian buyers, Feng Shui has become a necessary tool for the real estate, building, and business communities. Western culture can learn to embrace the concepts of common sense, beauty and functionality that work for everybody and include these in our living environments.

Within our communities there is a rising need to have central stabilizing forces. Sometimes these will be community centers, but they might also be a centrally located large home. The demographics of our population are changing rapidly. It is time for us to broaden our vision of the design needs of our future homes. A place that is designed to include safety features for disabled, elderly, and children, making all who enter feel welcome.

Many things are transforming this sense of space into home. Attitudes are changing. The demands of a home are more directed toward a place that encourages emotional expression and creativity. It expresses the new sense of the relationship between form and function. Its emphasis is on the meaning of place as well as the role of place.

The opportunity is here for us to create a place filled with sights, sounds, smells, tastes and textures to delight the senses. A place to experiment, to raise self esteem as well as children, an environment to mature body, mind and spirit, a place of "balance, order and beauty".

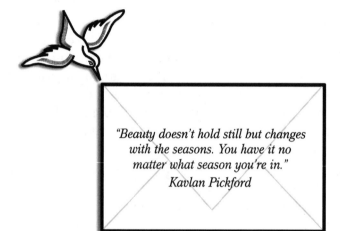

*"Beauty doesn't hold still but changes
with the seasons. You have it no
matter what season you're in."*
Kavlan Pickford

Simply Sacred Spaces

> "An altar is the perfect opportunity to express the goddess within. Your altar is your personal signature. People do subconscious altar building all the time. We call it interior decorating."
>
> Luisah Tiesh

Wish to do list

Is your home a sacred space for you? Can you relax when you enter? Are the objects you love enveloping you? Is there tranquillity, joy, and passion surrounding you? Does it nurture your soul?

Our haven we call home can be all the things we desire in life. We have the choice to create our own reality. Our attitude is the altimeter for the altitude we can achieve. The more optimistic about life we are the higher we can fly.

Do you dislike cleaning your space? Did you know that our everyday "chores" can be used to bring new meaning into our lives and give us inspiration? A change of attitude might help. There is a great deal of symbology in our homes. By creating rituals and ceremonies around this symbolism you can achieve delightful results.

For instance, the "chore" of cleaning a window can be an inspiring ritual for "creating a clear vision of the future," and removing clutter can be a ceremony of "out with the old, in with the new", thus giving birth to a new way of living life fully each day.

For example, to have a strong voice that is heard with authority, we need to have windows and mirrors clean and not chipped or cracked. Windows are symbolic of our vision and intentions in life. If the window is blocked, we may feel blocked in life. If it is cloudy, or dirty, we may not have a clear vision of either our purpose in life or how to package our God-given gifts for this world to see. If they are cracked or chipped, we may not feel whole or worthy of allowing the good to come to us, feeling we are not as perfect as we truly are.

By doing a ritual of cleaning windows, we become more clear as to our vision. By replacing or repairing them, we are taking a positive action to clear the negative belief system that has been reflected through the windows needing repair.

By drawing upon the knowledge and traditions of many cultures, including your own heritage, you can create a variety of techniques which can be used to bring in a new sense of simplicity and sacredness into your surroundings and life. This has been called "mindfulness."

To access the power we, as women have, we need to have a heightened awareness of our physical space. Everything in our lives is symbolic of various areas of our lives. Our dwellings are metaphorical for our bodies as well as life situations in our lives. There is an interrelationship of occupants, land, buildings, and furnishings.

Mirrors are a symbol of wealth and blessings in life. In Feng Shui, mirrors attract more good in life while repelling the bad or evil. There are many blessings, and the more we see, the more we can reflect them. Mirrors are a way to symbolize the reflection within each of us. So, finding a beautiful mirror and displaying it in an area of sacredness and spiritual power brings more of the same. Sarah Ban Breathnach in her book *Simple Abundance*, has called this the "Golden Mirror Meditation".

Doors are a symbol of the adult voice. If a door squeaks, you may not be taken seriously. If a door does not close properly, you may not have closure on issues that might be draining your energy. If there is clutter behind a closet door, there may be a cluttered life-style, lack of focus, etc.

Feminine power is gained by meandering lines, curved walkways, round and oval tables or objects. Masculine power is linear, logical, straight. We need both in our lives to be balanced. Most dwellings are linear (masculine/logical-yang energy), so we need to bring in the feminine (circular/intuitive-yin energy) chí, or energy.

To accept our sexual selves, we need to be comfortable with all sides of us; the yin-yang, soft-strong, light-dark (shadow) sides of us. We need places within our dwellings that reflect these opposites. We need a cave (dark, quiet place) to lick our wounds and heal. We need the meadow (open, joyful, beautiful, new growth place) to allow the light to shine on us and share that light. Where can it be created in our house?

In the bedroom we need to have both. Bringing in candles, the arrival of the new. Lastly, we want to ask that this Higher Power work through us to accomplish this. It's really very simple to bring the sacred into your home. Just ask!

Here are a couple more ideas to increase your well-being.

If you have a something you "won" in the divorce that has negative emotions or images for you, release it. The price you pay to keep it in your space is too high.

Check your emotional response to all your furnishings – furniture, plants, artwork, cards and gifts. If you do not love it, let it go!!!

As a gift to you in this book, I would like to share a very simple process to help you achieve the things you want to accomplish in and around your home. I call it my "Wish to Do List". As I discover something needs to be done around the house I write it on my list. This is not my "Honey-Do List" but a list I give to God to help me create in my life. These can be major repairs or minor items.

I list the job or item I want, the amount of money I think it will take to accomplish it, and the time I think it will take to physically complete the project. I ask, through prayer, for help and support, being fully aware of the many blessings I already have. As the item appears in my life, I put a Gold Star next to it. My "star-studded" list is a constant reminder of the many blessings God provides for me every day of my life.

Whether you're "Home Alone" or "Sharing with Children", we need to reinvent the home environment. Indigenous people understand the influence and power of the land and their physical environments. In our Western, materialistic world, many of us have lost or have never known the true essence of what a home can be.

There are many ceremonies or rituals you can do. Creating your own will make the most impact on your life. We can learn, play, and create when finding easy, low cost ways to improve our "sacred space". Through balance and harmony a person can change their life.

The Gift of the Red Envelope is a gift of peace, love, and wisdom to create a simply sacred space for you and your loved ones. It is simple to do, and a lovely, lifelong journey. Enjoy!

In Love and Light,
Linda Lenore

*If you would like to continue the tradition of **The Gift of the Red Envelope**, please share this knowledge with a friend and loved one. For the real riches of life come in all shapes, sizes and kinds of packaging. The gift of truth and wisdom is most empowering.*

Nine Design Enhancements

1) Bright or light-refracting objects:
   Mirrors/Pictures/Frames
   Crystal Balls/Cut Glass/Vases
   Lights/Candles/Night lights
2) Sounds:
   Wind Chimes
   Bells
   Music (Tapes, CD's, Instruments, Notes)
3) Living objects:
   Plants and flowers (real or realistic man-made) objects
   Aquariums or Fish Bowls
   Bird Feeders
   Nature or Natural Orientation
   Jewelry (Made from natural products, Look like living object)
4) Moving objects:
   Mobiles
   Windmills
   Fountains
5) Heavy objects (to stabilize):
   Stones
   Statues
   Houses (The Heart of the Home)
6) Electrically powered objects (to stimulate):
   Fountains
   Musical chimes
   Lights
   Diffusers
7) Fragrances/Smells
8) Color
9) Others (Delight the Little Child in **you** and **others**)

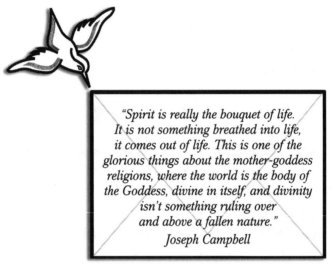

*"Spirit is really the bouquet of life.
It is not something breathed into life,
it comes out of life. This is one of the
glorious things about the mother-goddess
religions, where the world is the body of
the Goddess, divine in itself, and divinity
isn't something ruling over
and above a fallen nature."*
Joseph Campbell

Animal Energy in Artwork

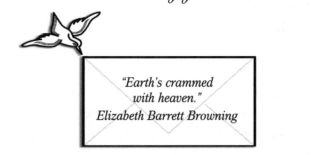

"Earth's crammed
with heaven."
Elizabeth Barrett Browning

It is essential for us to reconnect ourselves to the natural world verses the man-made world, to become one with heaven and earth. One way to do this is to incorporate more animals into our artwork, sculptures, statues, and fabric prints within our home. We can bring in the feeling of connection to the heavens through the energy of bird images and the connection to the earth through animals of the ground and water.

Energy of the Animals
from Land, Water and Air

Alligator: Aggression
   Survival
   Adaptability
Ant: Group minded
   Worker
Antelope: Speed and adaptability of the mind
Armadillo: Personal protection
   Discrimination
   Empathy
Ass: Wisdom
   Humility
Badger: Bold self-expression and Reliance
   Keeper of stories

Bat: Guardian of the night
 Cleaner
 Transition
 Initiation
Bear: Power
 Adaptability
 Awakening the power of the unconscious
Beaver: Builder
 Gatherer
 The building of dreams
Bluebird: Born to happiness
Bobcat: Silence and secrets
Buffalo: Sacredness
 Life
 Builder
 *Manifesting Abundance through right action and right
  prayer*
Bull: Fertility
Butterfly : Metamorphosis
 Creativity
 Change
 Clarity/Organization
 Carefree
 Transformer
Canary: Voice
Cardinal: Renew our own vitality
Cat: Mystery
 Magic
 Independence
Cockatoo: Friendship

Cougar: Leadership
Courage
Coming into your own power
Coyote: Prankster
Insight
Playful
Wisdom and folly
Crane: Longevity
Cuckoo: Listening skills
Deer: Love
Gentleness
Kindness
Innocence
Gentle luring to new adventure
Dogs: Loyalty
Security
Serving humanity
Loyal to own goals/values
Faithfulness
Protection
Dolphin: Breath of Life
Working with children
Joy
Barrier Breaker
Kindness
Play
Bridge man to ocean
The power of breath and sound
Doves: Peace
Dragonfly: Flighty
Carefree

Ducks: Home nurturing
Eagle: Divine spirit, Courage to Soar
    Connection to creator
    Whole brain thinking
    Balance in projects
    Hard work and completion of work
Echidna (Spiny anteater): Personal Boundaries
    Comfort zone
Elephant: Ancient power, strength, and royalty
Elk: Partnerships
    Pacing
    Camaraderie
    Support/Communication with your own gender
    Strength
    Agility
    Freedom
    Nobility
Fox: Cunning
    Provider
    Intelligence
    Feminine magic of camouflage, shape-shifting and
        invisibility
Frog : Connection with water element
Giraffe: Farsightedness
Goat: Surefootedness
    Seeking new heights
Goose: Mate for life
Grizzly: Bear Hunter
    Nature's pharmacist
Groundhog: Mystery of death without dying
    Trance

Dreams
Hawk: Protectors
Horse: Power
  Physical power (horse power)
  Wisdom
  Sharing knowledge
  Stamina
  Mobility
  Strength
  Travel
  Freedom
Hummingbird: see title page
Kangaroo: Abundance
  Family
Koala: Holding on
  Selectiveness
Leopard : Overcoming our demons and haunts
  Renewal
Lion : Assertion of the feminine and the power of the female sun
Lynx: Secrets and visions of the hidden and unseen
Lizard: Conservation
  Agility
Loon: Awakens dreams
Meadowlark: Cheerful journey inward
Moose: Headstrong
  Unstoppable
  Longevity
  Primal feminine energies
  The magic of life and death
Mouse: Attention to detail
Opossum: The use of appearances

Oriole: Sense of joy
Otter: Laughter
    Curiosity
    Mischievous
    Joy
    Playfulness
    Sharing
Owl: Higher wisdom
Panther: Reclaiming one's true power
Parrot: Link humans to bird kingdom
Pigeon: Homelife
Platypus: Camouflage
    Timidity
Porcupine: Renewed sense of wonder
Possum: Persistence
    Ego
Prairie Dog: Community
Quail: No hesitation during times of crises
Rabbit: Alertness
    Fertility
    New life
Raccoon: Dexterity
    Disguise
Ram: Seeking new beginnings
Rat: Success
    Restlessness
    Shrewdness
Raven: Birth and death
Rhinoceros: Ancient wisdom
Salmon: Instinct
    Persistence
    Determination

Seahorse: Confidence
    Grace
Sea Lions: Active imagination
    Adaptation
    Contentment
    Creativity
    Lucid Dreaming
Shark: Hunter
    Survival
Skunk: Sensuality
    Respect
    Self-esteem
Snake: Shrewdness
    Transformation
Spider: Creative
    Pattern of Life
Squirrel: Activity
    Preparedness
Stork: Children
Swan: Grace
    Balance
    Innocence
Tiger: Passion
    Power
    Devotion
    Sensuality
Turkey: Nourishment
Turtle: Self-contained
    Mother Earth
    Healing knowledge
    Creative source
Wombat: Survival
    Tenacity

"*I am aware of the splendor that ties*
All the things of the earth with the things
of the skies,
Here in my body the heavenly heat,
Here in my flesh the melodious beat
Of the plants that circle Divinity's feet."
Angela Morgan

Weasel: Sly
  Secret circumvention and/or pursuit
Whale: Wisdom
  Provider
  Cleanser
  Creation
  Power of song
  Awakening inner depths
Wolf : Teacher
  Forerunner of new ideas
  Part of a team
  Individual performance
  Loyalty
  Success
  Perseverance
  Guardianship
  Ritual
  Spirit

Energy of Woods for Use in the House

> *One generation plants the trees; another gets the shade.*
> Chinese Proverb

Ash: *Sensitivity*
    Higher Wisdom
Beech: *Tolerance*
    Softens criticism
Birch: *New beginnings*
    Cleansing the past
Cedar: *Healing*
    Protection
    Cleansing
Cherry: *New awakenings*
    Death and rebirth
Holly: *Protection*
Maple: *Promise*
    Balance
Oak: *Strength*
    Endurance
    Continuity
    Helpfulness
Palm: *Peace*
    Protection
Pine: *Creativity*
    Balance of emotions
Walnut: *"The road less traveled"*
    Transitions
Willow: *Inner vision and dreams*
    Healing

*"Continuity gives us roots;
change gives us branches,
letting us stretch and grow and
reach new heights."*
Pauline R. Kezer

Introduction to Aromatherapy

> "Let us be grateful to
> people who make us happy – they are
> the charming gardeners
> who make our souls blossom."
> Marcel Proust

Introduction & History

Today the term 'aromatherapy' seems to be on everyone's lips. It's on TV, in magazines such as Woman's Day, Family Circle, Prevention, Newsweek and at the cosmetic counter. So what is it?

Aromatherapy has been around for thousands of years. Before Christ was born the Egyptians, Greeks, Romans and others had been using the essences of plants in religious ceremonies, medicinally, cosmetically, and in daily life.

The term 'aromatherapy' was coined by the French chemist/perfumer GattefossE in 1928 and means "therapy using aromas." These aromas or essences are termed 'essential oils.' And aromatherapy is the art of using these oils.

The essential oils are the essences extracted from plants. They are part of the plant's own healing (immune) system. They are highly concentrated and contain vitamins, hormones, antiseptics and sometimes antifungal and antiviral properties.

Fragrance Oils

Essential oils should not be confused with many of the fragrance oils that are used in cosmetics, candles, air fresheners and house hold products. Fragrance oils are synthetic chemicals that are inorganic and though they may smell like a rose or sandalwood; they have only the smell, they do not have the other (possibly hundreds) components found in essential oils. Yes, they smell nice, but this is the same 'nice' that perfumes many of today's cleaning products. Essential oils contribute more than just perfume to our bodies. In choosing an 'aromatherapy' product check to see that it contains only 'essential oils' and not 'fragrance'.

Sense of Smell

Scientist are still discovering today that the sense of smell plays a decisive role in what we perceive, and that scents can cause various psychological and physical reactions. Our sense of smell is about 10,000 times more sensitive than our sense of taste. Aromas enter through the nose and pass directly into the brain into the limbic system. Here the aromatic information is stored with memories, pleasure, and emotions.

European researchers are finding that aromatherapy does work. Recent studies have found that lavender promotes sleep, and that peppermint helps headaches. And researchers are now testing the use of rosemary on patients in the early stages of Alzheimer's disease.

Essential Oils - How They Work

Essential oils affect the body, mind and spirit. Much as they work in plants, they stimulate human metabolism and transmit neurochemical "messages" to organs (skin), glands (hormones), or body systems (lymphatic, blood circulation, immune system).

They are antibacterial - killing and preventing germs ,and some are also antiviral and/or antifungal.

Essential Oils are different from the "fatty" oils (olive, almond, peanut, etc.) that we're familiar with. They are highly volatile, fragrant, substances. Fatty oils do make an excellent compliment to essential oils and will be discussed further later.

Essential oils are extracted from: roots, bark, flower, leaf, seed, fruit and resin of plants.

The method used of extracting essential oils is usually determined by how much oil can be extracted and the price of the extraction process.

Distillation - steam passes though the plant material carrying the essential oil and water with it, the oil is then separated (lavender, chamomile), and the water is sometimes used as a facial mist, this water is called a hydrosol.

Cold pressing - the essential oil is extracted by shredding, scraping, squeezing or pressing the oil from the plant (citrus oils).

Absolute through enfleurage - oils are extracted into fat, then alcohol is added to separate the essential oil from the fat (rose, jasmine).

Absolute through chemical solvent - the plant is immersed in a mineral solvent (i.e. hexane) which produces a solid (concrete). It is then treated with alcohol to extract the essential oil.

Resinoid (or oleoresin) - extracts from heavy gums or resins the aromatic matter (alcohol is also usually used) (frankincense).

Carbon dioxide (CO) - essential oils are extracted under high pressure without chemicals or solvents (this is a new process).

Care of Essential Oils

Essential oils are very concentrated, they can be 70 to 100 times more potent that the plant. Because they are so concentrated you only need to use drops. They should be respected and used carefully.

THEY SHOULD ALWAYS BE OUT OF THE REACH OF CHILDREN!!!

Essential oils evaporate in the air with varying speeds and intensities. The oils are highly sensitivity to light and heat. Store them in tightly capped dark bottles (amber or blue bottles are good). They should not be stored in plastic containers, since the chemicals in the plastics can interact with the essential oils.

Essential oils, pricing

The cost of oils can be puzzling.

Why does 1/3 ounce of orange cost a few dollars, 1/2 ounce of lavender cost over $10 and 1/16 of an ounce of rose over $20?

The difference in price is caused by 3 main factors. The first is how many pounds of the plant are needed to produce the oil.

1/3 ounce of oil is produced by:

8.8 pounds of clary sage

22 pounds of rosemary

1,110 pounds of rose petals

2,200 pounds of hyacinth blossoms

Second, some woods and plants are becoming more rare. Recently the Indian government has reduced the amount of sandalwood that can be cut and exported.

And thirdly, there may be political reasons such as wars or embargoes.

Be careful and read the labels of the oils you buy. Some companies mix essential oils with carrier oils to decrease their price. Also, some oils are artificial and not 'essential oils,' rose oil for $3.99 for 1/4 ounce is not real rose!

Aromatherapy Oils & Uses

The following is a list of some essential oils and their properties:

Basil - warm and spicy; derived from the leaves and flowers of the sweet basil plant. Very potent, use sparingly, it's a mental stimulant also used for coughs, congestion, and headaches (avoid if you are pregnant).

Bergamot - spicy citrus; derived from the peel of the fruit of the Italian tree, Citrus Bergamia. Uplifting and refreshing; it can be inhaled to soothe your digestion and nervousness. Because bergamot is a photosensitizer it should not be used for skin applications if you will be out in the sun. It can also be an irritant to sensitive skin.

Birch - pungent and woody; derived from the bark of the US and Canadian Birch tree. Especially good in the bath or a massage oil for muscular aches and pains. Also an external diuretic and cleanser. The oil from Birch buds is used in shampoos, scalp treatments, and dandruff. It is also used externally in lotions for healing skin irritations.

Cedarwood - woody, from the trunk of the American Cedar tree. Used as a nerve tonic, respiration and hair care. Used in massage, diffusers, and shampoo/conditioners.

Chamomile (German or Roman) – dry with a slight sweetness. Distilled from the flowers. It is calming, used externally for digestive upsets, headaches, menstrual cramps, and anti-inflammatory in skin care. It is used as a hair tonic to stimulate growth or on the skin to stimulate the complexion.

Clary Sage - herbal, nutty, slightly sweet. Distilled from flowers and leaves. Used in massage it is considered uplifting, also for muscular aches, pains and menstrual cramps. It also supports the respiratory and digestive systems. Also used for hair and body care products; for acne, dandruff, oily skin, and hair loss.

Eucalyptus - dry, warming. Distilled from the tree. Used for the respiratory system, it is also antiseptic and also may aid some headaches. When used in a vaporizer it is effective in killing bacteria and aids coughs, colds and bronchial infections. It has also been shown to be effective for herpes, sinus headaches, muscular aches and pains.

Frankincense Oil - steam distilled from frankincense resin. One of the first oils used in rituals. It is antiseptic, astringent and tonic. It is used externally for skin afflictions such as boils and pimples. And for respiratory ailments as an inhalant for bronchitis, colds and coughs. Inhaling the vapors of Frankincense soothes the spirit and deepens the breath, this is probably why it has been used for meditation and prayer.

Geranium (Rose) - is derived from the flowers and leaves of the Rose pelargonium. It is used in creams and ointments for healing the skin. When diffused the scent is an antidepressant, relaxing but a stimulant to the psyche. It is said to have cellular regenerative properties and is good in anti-wrinkle creams.

Jasmine - rich, floral, warming and uplifting. It is distilled from the flowers. It is antidepressant, anti-inflammatory, antiseptic, aphrodisiac and good for dry, irritated sensitive skin. It is one of the more expensive oils (about $25.00 for 1/16 ounce) it is best to use in massage or for facial creams.

Lavender - floral, slightly sweet and spicy from the flower. Used in general first aid, burns, bites, headaches, insomnia. Used in baths, massage, perfume, diffuser. Good during pregnancy.

Lemon - sweet, fresh, citrus, pressed from the skin. It is antiseptic, antirheumatic, astringent, diuretic and stimulates white corpuscles. Used for acne, corns, throat infections, 'flu and fever. Also in massage oils for high blood pressure, arthritis, rheumatism, colds and poor circulation.

Marjoram - smells green and slightly sweet. Extracted from the flower,. Good for headaches and for the digestive system (externally in massage, not internally), calms the nerves – (avoid if pregnant).

Patchouli - earthy sweet, antibiotic, antifungal, antidepressive, inspiration. Used in perfumes, body oils, salves and in diffusers.

Peppermint - extracted from the leaf, green and refreshing. Used for the digestive system (externally), for headaches, travel sickness. It is cooling and invigorating (great for tired feet as a foot bath or oil).

Pine - sweet, dry, balsamic scent. Distilled from the needles. Analgesic, antirheumatic, antiseptic, bactericidal, expectorant, insecticidal, stimulant. Used for circulation, muscles, joints, bronchitis, coughs, sinusitis, urinary infections, colds, 'flu, nervous exhaustion, stress and insecticidal (lice).

Rose - floral and heady, is said to be an aphrodisiac (opens the heart spiritually). Used for skin care, may be good for headaches and hangovers (supports the liver, but use sparingly). Another very expensive oil especially depending on how it is extracted (for 1/16 ounce about $22.00 if extracted using solvents, about $53.00 if extracted without solvents).

Rosemary - it is green and invigorating. It is distilled from the leaf and flower. It is a mental stimulant, aids the liver, oily skin care, and low blood pressure. Avoid if pregnant or high blood pressure and do not use for long periods of time.

Sandalwood - warm and woody, from the wood of the Sandalwood tree. Used for nervous tension, supports the respiratory system and the skin. Used in perfumes, salves, massage, baths, shampoos/conditioner.

Tea Tree - from the leaf, pungent, antiseptic, antibacterial, antifungal. Used in first aid, cuts, bites, athletes foot, warts; in salves or compresses. When diffused purifies the air.

Ylang Ylang - heavy and floral. Extracted from the flower. Used as a relaxant, dispels anger, euphoric, aphrodisiac, balancing, induces sleep. Is used in skin care for oily skin.

Diffusers

Diffusion is a way of putting the essential oils into the air. Some of the methods of diffusion are:

Put the oil in a very warm pan or cup of water, it will diffuse into the air.

Using a unlit candle place some oil into the 'well' of the candle then light the candle. The heat from the candle will send the oil into the air.

Lamp rings are a circular ring made of metal, ceramic or other material that will sit on top of a light bulb. Place 4 to 6 drops of the oil on (or in) the ring and turn the light on.

Some diffusers have a heat source (candle or electricity) on the bottom and then a small bowl for the oil on top. It's a good idea to use some water with the oil (about 1 tablespoon of water and 4 to 6 drops of oil).

Also, there are ceramic containers that are usually small pots or figurines that are unglazed (partially or entirely). Oil is put in or on them and the air carries the scent. These are very effective in small places such as a cubicle, closet, car or drawer.

Lastly, there are nebulizers, that have electric pumps which take a vial of oil and spritz a micro-fine mist of the oil into the air. These tend to be the most expensive.

Note - with an electric model you can plug it into a timer and have the diffuser turned on for a certain occasion; before bedtime, for awakening, etc..

Carrier Oils & Uses

Carrier oils is the term used in aromatherapy for vegetable oils that are used with the essential oils. They help spread the essential oils onto the skin and act as a buffer for potent oils which used alone may burn the skin.

For dry skin: almond oil, avocado oil, olive and cocoa butter.

For normal skin: Jojoba, sesame oil, apricot kernel oil

For oily skin: walnut oil, sunflower oil, grapeseed oil and Hazelnut oil.

Do not use mineral oil as it coats the skin and blocks out the essential oil(s).

Useful Measurements

1 ml = 20 drops
5 ml = 1 tsp.
30 ml = 1 fl. oz.
500 ml = 8.45 oz
1 dram = 1/16 oz
1 dram = 1.875 ml

Important rule:

Success in skin care results not from using large amounts of essential oils or mixing many oils together, but rather from using a small mixture of the right oils.

Some Suggested Uses:

Except for Lavender and Tea Tree (for wounds, cold sores and warts), DO NOT use essential oils directly on the skin always dilute in water, oil or cremes. Most of the oils can be a skin irritant, please handle with care.

Massages – for each ounce of massage oil use 4 to 10 drops. Because the oil is going to be used on a large area of the body, start with a little and don't perfume all of the oil at once.

Facial Spray – in 4 ounces of distilled/spring water, use about 4 to 6 drops.

Bath – use 6 to 10 drops.

Body Lotion – use 4 to 6 drops per ounce of lotion, depending on how 'perfumed' you like it.

Cold or the flu, or sinusitus – use a few drops of Eucalyptus in a pan of hot water, create a tent with a towel over you and the pan (be careful not to burn yourself) and inhale the fumes for a few minutes.

Scenting a room – In a candle diffuser or lamp-ring diffuser use about 3-6 drops for the room.

Wake up – bath with Rosemary or Lemongrass (4 to 6 drops).

Mental fatigue – Basil, put a drop or two on a tissue and inhale. Soothing Lavender, in the bath (4 to 6 drops), or a couple of drops on a tissue.

Jet-lag – a bath with a couple of drops of Ylang-Ylang and Lavender for a restful sleep.

Emotional uplift – try a few drops of Clary Sage, Orange or Tangerine in a bath, diffuser or tissue.

Aching feet – a few drops of Rosemary, Peppermint or Lavender in oil (olive oil is fine).

Insomnia – put a few drops of Lavender or Neroli onto your pillowcase or tissue.

Avoidance

High blood pressure – hyssop, rosemary, sage and thyme

Epilepsy – fennel, sage, thuja and hyssop

Pregnancy – basil, camphor, carrot seed, cedarwood, clove, frankincense, hyssop, juniper, myrrh, oregano, rosemary, sage, lemon verbena, pennyroyal, and sassafras. Many herbalists recommend to not use aromatherapy oils during the first trimester, ALWAYS consult with your doctor.

Remember in working with oils, to choose those that appeal to you.

Aromatherapy information provided by Irene Jacobson,
The Herbal Home, Menlo Park, California
http://www.herbalhome.com

Sources for this information

Rose, Jeanne. The Aromatherapy Book North Atlantic Books, 1992

Ody, Penelope. The Complete Medicinal Herbal. Dorling Kindersley, 1993

Lawless, Julia. The Illustrated Encyclopedia of Essential Oils. Element Books Inc., 1995

Keville, Kathy. Herbs An Illustrated Encyclopedia. Friedman/Fairfax Publishing, 1994

House Blessing
by
Carol Nosko

I offer you this candle
that light may shine within and without
every room of your home.
I offer this bread and wine
for the deepening of spirit and union
with all gatherings around your table.
I offer this coin
as symbol of continued blessings and joy
for all who live and enter
this gracious dwelling.

These symbolic gifts are offered in many cultures as
a house blessing.

Salt is used in the Jewish tradition instead of bread
and wine.

Bibliography

Andrews, Ted. *Animals Speak*, 1993 by Llewellyn Publications.

Anderson, Peggy. *Great Quotes From Great Women*, 1992
by Successories Publishing.

Ban Breathnach, Sarah. *Simple Abundance*, 1995 by Warner Books, Inc..

Ban Breathnach, *The Simple Abundance Journal of Gratitude*, 1996
by Warner Books, Inc.

Beinfield, Harriet and Efrem Korngold. *Between Heaven and Earth*,
1985 by Ballantine Books.

Boates, Karen Scott. *The Goddess Within*, 1990 by Running Press.

Brennan, Barbara Ann. *Hands of Light*, 1987 by Bantam Books.

Dossey, Larry, M.D. *Healing Words*, 1993 by Harper San Francisco.

Eisler, Riane, *The Chalice and The Blade: Our History, Our Future*,
1987 by HarperCollins.

Estes, Clarissa Pinkola, Ph.D. *Women Who Run With the Wolves*, 1992
by Ballantine Books.

Hammerschlag, Carl A., M.D. *The Dancing Healers*, 1989
by Harper & Row.

Hay, Louise L. *Heal Your Body*, 1988 by Hay House.

Hill, Napolean. *The Think and Grow Rich Action Pack*, 1972
by Plume Books.

Hoyt, Maureen. *Creative Thought*, 1998 by Religious Science International.

Lawlor, Anthony. *The Temple in the House*, 1994
by G. P. Putnam's Sons.

Liberman, Jacob, Ph.D. *Light*, 1991 by Bear & Company.

Linn, Denise. *Sacred Space*, 1995 by Ballantine Books.

Lip, Evelyn, *Feng Shui*, 1987 by Heian International, Inc.

Litt, Iris F., M.D. *Taking Our Pulse*, 1997 by Stanford University Press.

Mandino, Og. *A Better Way to Live*, 1990 by Bantam Books.

McClelland, Carol L., Ph.D. *The Seasons of Change*, 1998
by Conari Press.

Meadows, Kenneth. *The Medicine Way*, 1990 by Element Books.

Moore, Thomas. *Care of the Soul*, 1992 by HarperPerennial.

Murphy, Pat, *By Nature's Design*, 1993 by Chronicle Books.

Nabokov, Peter and Robert Easton, **Native American Architecture**, 1989 by Oxford University Press.

National Association of Professional Organizers, San Francisco Bay Area Chapter. **Organizing Options**, 1994 by National Association of Professional Organizers.

Pearson, David. **The Natural House Book**, 1989 by Fireside Books.

Rees, Alwyn and Brinley. **Celtic Heritage**, 1961 by Thames and Hudson, Inc.

Rinpoche, Sogyal. **The Tibetan Book of Living and Dying**, 1993 by Harper San Francisco.

Rossbach, Sarah. **Feng Shui**, 1983 by E.P. Dutton, Inc.

Rossbach, Sarah. **Interior Design with Feng Shui**, 1987 by E.P. Dutton, Inc.

Rossbach, Sarah and Lin Yun. **Living Color**, 1994 by Kodansha International, Limited.

Roszak, Theodore, Mary E. Gomes, and Allen D. Kanner. **Ecopsycology**, 1995 by Sierra Club Books.

Running Press. **Home**, 1996 by Running Press Miniature Edition.

Spear, William. **Feng Shui Made Easy**, 1995 by Harper San Francisco.

Stone, Jana. **Every Part of This Earth Is Sacred**, 1993 by Harper San Francisco.

Troward, Thomas. **Bible Mystery and Bible Meaning**, 1992 by DeVorss Publications.

Warner, Carolyn. **Treasury of Womenis Quotations**, 1992 by Prentice-Hall, Incorporated.

Williams-Fitzgerald, Ann and Karen Osborn. **Wisdom of the Australian Animals**, by Hihouse Publishing Party Limited.

Williamson, Maria. **A Womanis Worth**, 1993 by Random House.

Order & Contact Information

Orders and information can be directed to the address or phone number below.

Learn about the philosophy of Feng Shui and how to use the Ba-Gua to balance your life.

"Change your Environment, Change your Life"
Audio Cassette – $9

Discover the metaphor of home as levels of interaction with people to learn ways to enhance relationships.

Book – $18
Nurturing the Soul Video – $27

Look for Linda's next book:
The First Gift of the Red Envelope

Linda Lenore
A Beautiful Center of Light
P.O. Box 7656
Menlo Park, C 94026
650-368-5532
http://www.lindalenore.com

Linda Lenore is the founder of *Interior Spaces,* a design firm, and *A Beautiful Center of Light,* an educational and research organization. She travels internationally teaching continuing education classes on Feng Shui and creating sacred spaces to the design community through the American society of Interior Designers (ASID) and at colleges and universities. She creates "Harmonious Homes", "Balance, Order and Beauty", and "Simply Sacred Spaces" through workshops by those names.

As a keynote speaker, she inspires her audiences to find the "pearl of great price" in their life to help them through transitions while she integrates knowledge of cultural beliefs and stories of real life, hers and others. She is a member of the National Association of Professional Organizers (NAPO), National Speakers Association (NSA), Ozark Research Institute (ORI), an affiliate member of ASID, and a 1998 graduate of Redwood City/San Carlos/Belmont Leadership.